Praise for

"Like having lunch with your new best friend, the one who sees you not just as you are but as you could be, *Burn Your Sh*t* is wise and tender, witty and insightful—and an indispensable manual for building transformative ritual into your life in practical, accessible ways. For those who have been transformed by writers like Glennon Doyle, Cheryl Strayed, and Jen Sincero, please add Lori Dyan to your reading list now as a next step on your journey to the very place you were always meant to arrive."
—Marissa Stapley, *New York Times* bestselling author of *Lucky*

"With a blend of delightful humor and spiritual wisdom, *Burn Your Sh*t* invites the reader into practicing rituals with ease and intention. Through her words, Lori Dyan blends magic with concrete practicality to help us bridge two worlds. Whether you consider yourself a beginner or have been practicing ceremony for decades, *Burn Your Sh*t* offers brilliant ritual advice for modern times."
—Asha Frost, Indigenous healer and bestselling author of *You Are the Medicine* and *The Sacred Medicine Oracle Deck*

"Lori is special. Those who know just know and you feel it when you get time with her. Her insight is beautiful, inspiring, and reminds you that your intuition is a guiding light. On top of all of this, her humor is another piece that sets her apart."
—Cheryl Hickey, Canadian TV personality

"This book is lightning in a bottle. Lori brings her vitality, wisdom, and wit to help us transform our lives through the power of ritual. She provides the tools and the spark to help us 'set fire to our limiting beliefs.' This beauty of a book is a bridge to our own soulful evolution. It's a healing path on the page. Dive in."
—Heidi Rose Robbins, astrologer, poet, and author of *Everyday Radiance: 365 Zodiac Prompts for Self-Care and Self-Renewal*

"*Burn Your Sh*t* is an amazing guide. I've had the pleasure of working with Lori to bring more rituals into my life, impacting positive change for the highest good of myself and others!"
—Nyakio Grieco, co-founder of Thirteen Lune and founder of Relevant Skin

"This is my kind of book! Life-changing rituals done with a practical approach? Count me in! Lori Dyan takes us step-by-step to creating an important element of our spiritual practice with the help of powerful rituals that work for you. Lori is a brilliant and talented tarot reader and teacher who gifts us all with information we need to create our own authentic rituals that can help transform our lives. From crystals to cauldrons, Lori thoughtfully and humorously explains the origins, reasons, and purposes of these powerful mystical techniques. If you are looking to be out with the old and in with the new, clean up your energy, or just wanting to elevate your inner witch, this is the book for you!"
—MaryAnn DiMarco, author of *Medium Mentor: 10 Powerful Techniques to Awaken Divine Guidance for Yourself and Others*, internationally recognized psychic medium, and speaker

BIG
DECK
ENERGY

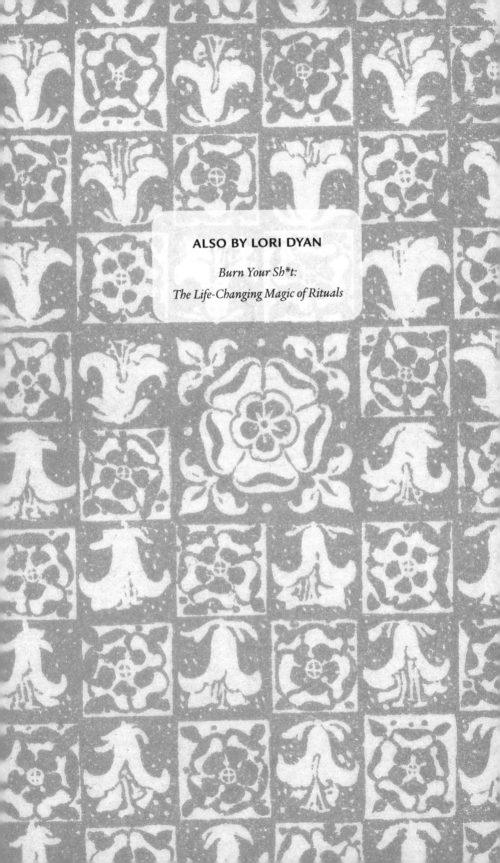

ALSO BY LORI DYAN

*Burn Your Sh*t:
The Life-Changing Magic of Rituals*

BIG DECK ENERGY

THE LIFE-CHANGING WISDOM OF TAROT

∞

LORI DYAN

Collins
An Imprint of HarperCollinsPublishersLtd

Big Deck Energy
Copyright © 2025 by Lori Dyan.
All rights reserved.

Published by Collins, an imprint of HarperCollins Publishers Ltd

First Edition

This publication contains the opinions and ideas of its author. This publication is not intended to provide a basis for action in particular circumstances. Prior to conducting any fire ritual, all appropriate fire safety issues should be taken into account, including all applicable fire regulations in the relevant jurisdiction. The author and publisher expressly disclaim any responsibility for any liability, loss, or risk, personal or otherwise, that is incurred as a consequence, directly or indirectly, of the use and application of any of the contents of this book.

QR codes and third-party internet addresses were accurate at the time the book went to press, and the author and publisher are not responsible for any changes to them.

No part of this book may be used or reproduced in any manner whatsoever without written permission.

Art on page 1: ©gomixer/stock.adobe.com
Rider-Waite tarot cards in the public domain, created by Pamela Colman Smith

Without limiting the author's and publisher's exclusive rights, any unauthorized use of this publication to train generative artificial intelligence (AI) technologies is expressly prohibited.

HarperCollins books may be purchased for educational, business, or sales promotional use through our Special Markets Department.

HarperCollins Publishers Ltd
Bay Adelaide Centre, East Tower
22 Adelaide Street West, 41st Floor
Toronto, Ontario, Canada
M5H 4E3

www.harpercollins.ca

HarperCollins Publishers
Macken House, 39/40 Mayor Street Upper
Dublin 1, D01 C9W8, Ireland
https://www.harpercollins.com

Library and Archives Canada Cataloguing in Publication

Title: Big deck energy : the life-changing wisdom of tarot / Lori Dyan.
Names: Dyan, Lori, author.
Description: Includes bibliographical references.
Identifiers: Canadiana (print) 20250161788 | Canadiana (ebook) 20250163462 | ISBN 9781443471589 (softcover) | ISBN 9781443471596 (ebook)
Subjects: LCSH: Tarot. | LCSH: Tarot cards. | LCSH: Self-actualization (Psychology) | LCGFT: Self-help publications.
Classification: LCC BF1879.T2 D93 2025 | DDC 133.3/2424—dc23

Printed and bound in the United States of America

25 26 27 28 29 LBC 5 4 3 2 1

To my tarot deck, for everything

Contents

∞

Preface 1
Introduction 3
CHAPTER 1: Tarot Before TikTok
         (A Brief History) 7
CHAPTER 2: Woo Woo Without the Cuckoo
         (How Tarot Works) 17
CHAPTER 3: Hit the Deck
         (How to Choose & Care for Your Cards) 27
CHAPTER 4: Tarot Tinder
         (Getting to Know Your Cards) 41
CHAPTER 5: Therapy in a Box
         (Tarot as a Self-Help Tool) 51
CHAPTER 6: Be Your Own Psychic
         (Tarot & Intuition) 59

CONTENTS

CHAPTER 7: Don't Be a Dick
    (The Ethics & Etiquette of Tarot)   69

CHAPTER 8: Fools & Kings for Ding-a-Lings
    (Arcana Architecture)   79

CHAPTER 9: Towers & Devils & Death, Oh My!
    (The Major Arcana)   91

CHAPTER 10: Hot Rods
    (Wands)   141

CHAPTER 11: Bottoms Up
    (Cups)   159

CHAPTER 12: Pointy Parts
    (Swords)   181

CHAPTER 13: Get That Bag
    (Pentacles/Coins)   199

CHAPTER 14: Have a Conversation with Your Soul
    (Readings)   217

CHAPTER 15: Sticks & Stars
    (Tarot & Astrology)   241

CHAPTER 16: Spread 'Em
    (Putting It All Together)   251

Conclusion   267
Acknowledgments   269

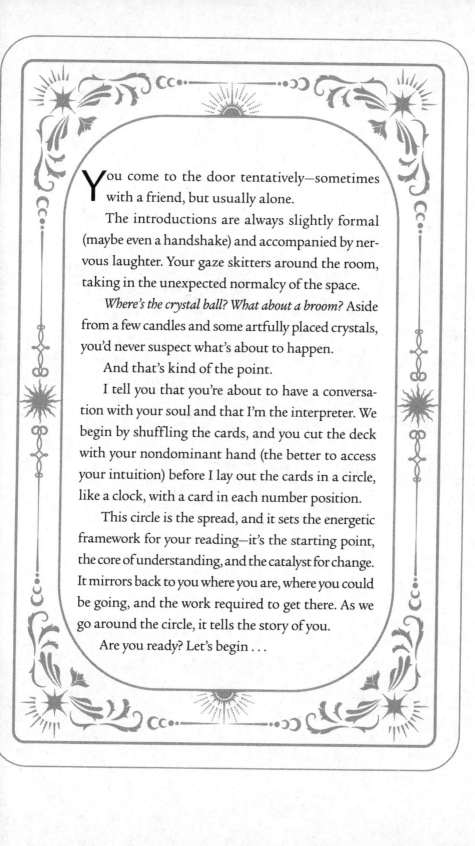

You come to the door tentatively—sometimes with a friend, but usually alone.

The introductions are always slightly formal (maybe even a handshake) and accompanied by nervous laughter. Your gaze skitters around the room, taking in the unexpected normalcy of the space.

Where's the crystal ball? What about a broom? Aside from a few candles and some artfully placed crystals, you'd never suspect what's about to happen.

And that's kind of the point.

I tell you that you're about to have a conversation with your soul and that I'm the interpreter. We begin by shuffling the cards, and you cut the deck with your nondominant hand (the better to access your intuition) before I lay out the cards in a circle, like a clock, with a card in each number position.

This circle is the spread, and it sets the energetic framework for your reading—it's the starting point, the core of understanding, and the catalyst for change. It mirrors back to you where you are, where you could be going, and the work required to get there. As we go around the circle, it tells the story of you.

Are you ready? Let's begin . . .

Introduction

∞

My name is Lori, and I'm a professional tarot card reader, known through my work as Tarot Lori. I've been doing it for thirty-five years using my original deck, and I work with clients around the world—from Alaska to Australia and Kenya to Kuwait—to inspire, empower, and enlighten them with tarot.

I call my unique brand of tarot "Woo Woo Without the Cuckoo" because it gives a sense of my approach to reading cards. I obviously do this for a living and take it very seriously, but I'm not goofy about it. You won't find me in a tacky costume, staring at you awkwardly as I make gimmicky predictions. And I'll never tell you to say goodbye to the dog or anything scary like that. But I may blow your mind with how randomly specific tarot cards can be.

I've always been interested in metaphysical matters (aka woo woo), but growing up in Calgary, Alberta, in the 80s didn't offer much in the way of resources. There was only one store that sold card decks and crystals (along with bongs and rolling papers), and psychics were found through word of mouth. That's how I discovered Erica—a legit broom-toting, spell-casting, crystal ball–gazing witch.

It felt like coming home.

Erica did psychic readings using tarot, and her approach was relatable and reassuring; she never used tarot cards to scare people, but she didn't shy away from the heavy stuff either. Although her gravity-defying platinum beehive, goth makeup, and Stevie Nicks–inspired wardrobe could be intimidating, she was an absolute sweetheart who eventually became my tarot mentor. (Fun fact: The spread that I discuss in Chapter 16 evolved from one she created.)

When I finally got my own deck, I had no clue what I was doing and would give "readings" to friends. These consisted of my pulling a card and then checking the little guidebook that came with the deck (with notes crammed in the margins from my sessions with Erica). "It says this card means that..." I'd mutter. "Does that make *any* sense to you?" We would stare at each other, me desperate for validation and my friend completely confused.

The best thing that ever happened—aside from being mentored by a bona fide witch—was losing the instruction book in my early twenties. If I wanted to continue reading tarot cards, I was on my own.

I had only vague recollections of tarot definitions and was forced to rely on my intuition. The internet wasn't invented yet, so no googling for me. What initially felt terrifying (doing tarot without a net) ended up being incredibly liberating. When I found the guidebook a few years later, I realized I no longer needed it. My cards had started telling stories that didn't always align with standard tarot definitions but accessed deep truths. These messages were being channeled. The only proof I needed was how they resonated with the person being read, and how helpful and hopeful, rather than cheesy or chilling, my readings became.

Despite my obsession with tarot, it took years for me to consider it a career. But through every stage of my adult life, from university student to corporate bigwig, tarot was my constant. I offered readings anywhere to anyone, and my cards kept me from getting fired from at least two jobs—I would take clients to lunch and give them readings instead of talking shop. (This was for the best because I never really understood the "shop" part.)

Eventually, people started to seek me out after hearing about "Lori who does tarot" (which became "Tarot Lori"). I started doing readings for groups and called them "Spiritual Soirées." I was asked to teach my style of tarot, so I led workshops at metaphysical stores and in my home studio.

During this time, just as writers develop a signature voice, I was unconsciously cultivating my specific approach to tarot—one that fulfilled my intention to give readings that inspire, empower, and enlighten—in a way that reflected my sense of humor and storytelling style.

A lot has happened since my first reading with Erica, and my life has taken some interesting turns, but tarot has always been my North Star, guiding me home to myself.

My deck contains every reading I've ever done, and after thousands of them, I know what it takes to become a confident and insightful tarot card reader. I've seen what's possible when you learn how to read the cards intuitively, and I've also seen what happens when they're used as a scare tactic or TikTok prop.

The thought of memorizing seventy-eight cards is daunting and totally unnecessary. I'm here to help you develop and deepen an authentic relationship with your deck in a way that isn't complicated or scary. I've taught thousands of people just like you how to gain a very personal and profound connection to tarot. You'll be getting more than standard Tarot 101 definitions because those can be found online for free. Instead, I'll be providing my interpretations—developed over decades—and show you how the teachings of tarot can be found in everyday life, every single day. You'll get practical strategies and proven techniques for crafting the perfect question, what goes into the ideal spread, and other tips I've picked up over the past thirty-five years.

This book is more than a resource for reading tarot: It's a how-to guide for doing life. We're going to reframe what is possible with the cards and look at how you can integrate them into your self-help tool kit.

Together, we'll put these ancient teachings into practice so you can work with your cards to see opportunities and challenges with clarity, determine the right direction, inspire healing in your heart and soul, demolish outdated narratives and unhelpful patterns, and transition to a place of endless possibilities where you can discover your purpose and step into your potential. (And also so you can whip your cards out at a party and blow everyone's mind because tarot is *very* fun and incredibly cool.)

You're about to embark on a pathway to self-discovery with the cards as your map. We were all newbies once, and I hope to be one of many teachers you encounter on your tarot journey.

CHAPTER 1

∞

Tarot Before TikTok
(A Brief History)

Tarot is seen by some as a New Age cliché alongside astrology or crystal healing, but as with our fascination with the stars above us and the rocks beneath our feet, there's nothing "new" about tarot.

Tarot dates back hundreds of years, and while people have assigned it to different cultures and eras, the truth is that nobody knows for certain when tarot was developed or who was responsible. But there are a *lot* of theories.

The origin story of the deck you're familiar with today is layered in conjecture and hypotheticals disguised as legends and myths. Some people claim that tarot artwork is encrypted with the ancestral wisdom of ancient civilizations, while others believe the imagery was born from the Roman festival of saturnalia. The oldest surviving tarot deck (although incomplete) is the gold-leaf *Visconti-Sforza* tarot, and it dates back to fifteenth-century Italy, but its provenance is shrouded in mystery. A lot of what you hear depends on the source, with lots of fables and very few facts.

Historians can't even agree on where the word "tarot" comes from. Many cite the Italian word *"tarocchi,"* which comes from a traditional card game. Another version insists that it's derived from Egyptian roots: *"Tar"* (path) and *"Ro"* (royal). The connection between ancient Egypt and tarot was promoted in the eighteenth century by a French occultist (we'll get to him in a minute), but there are compelling ideas about how tarot really came to Italy.

THE SILK ROAD

Although China is known as the birthplace of playing cards, first referenced during the tenth century, those cards had no numerical values and bore little resemblance to modern playing cards. It isn't until the Mamluk Sultanate of Egypt (1250–1517) that we find evidence of cards numbered ace through ten, along with a few court cards added to the mix. Most notably, there were also four distinct suits—curved swords, polo sticks, cups, and coins.

Due to Islamic law prohibiting the depiction of human images, the intricate design of the Mamluk cards lacks the storytelling imagery associated with tarot, but these cards are a commonly accepted link between earlier cards from Asia and the genesis of playing cards in Europe because they share a number of similarities. Early examples of Mamluk cards adapted to suit European tastes have been found preserved inside old books, used to stiffen the book covers.

It's most likely that playing cards were transported along trade routes from Asia to Egypt, eventually making their way to Europe in the late 1300s, where the earliest iterations of tarot decks can be found (although they were still used as playing cards in parlor games—it's unclear who first used tarot cards for divination, or when exactly it happened). The oldest complete tarot deck is the *Sola-Busca* tarot from the late 1400s; this Italian deck contains the structure of a modern tarot deck, with fifty-six suit cards (Minor Arcana) and twenty-two trump cards (Major Arcana).

THE ULTIMATE STATUS SYMBOL

Once playing cards landed in Europe, they were incredibly popular with aristocrats because they were handmade, intricately painted works of art—if a family commissioned a deck, you knew they were fancy AF.

In addition to being shown off, the cards were used to play games like *Carte da trionfi* and *Tarocchi Appropriati* (similar to bridge or poker), but their vibrant imagery and vivid symbolism soon attracted the attention of mystics and paranormal practitioners who reimagined the cards as a tool for divination.

Although playing cards have evolved significantly over the past few hundred years, with countless variations that included early tarot imagery and structure, particular moments indicate tarot's transition from card game to metaphysical mainstay, starting in France during the 1700s.

WHAT'S THE FRENCH WORD FOR "WOO WOO"?

The mythology of tarot and its ties to esotericism were forged in France throughout the eighteenth and nineteenth centuries. Tarot symbolism was reinterpreted to reflect the sensibilities of the era, and French people in the 1700s were equally fascinated by Egypt (in part because Napoleon was obsessed with conquering it) and the Hebrew system of mystical esoteric teachings known as Kabbalah.

In 1781, Antoine Court de Gébelin, a former Protestant minister, published *Le Monde Primitif*, a speculative history of tarot that proposed a complex system for using tarot to predict the future.

Gébelin declared that symbols found in France's *Tarot de Marseille*, published in the 1500s, contained wisdom that could be traced back to holy scriptures written by Egyptian priests. He further asserted that the illustrations of the Major Arcana contained hidden mysteries from the legend of Isis as well as the *Book of Thoth*, a synthesis of sacred wisdom from the Ptolemaic period (332–30 BCE) of ancient Greece written in a form of hieroglyphics.

It all sounds very magical and sexy, but the problem with Gébelin is that he had no factual or historical evidence to support his claims. At the time of his writing, hieroglyphics were indecipherable, and once Egyptologists *could* read them, nothing was found to verify Gébelin's tall tarot tales. He also alleged that tarot cards were brought to Europe from Egypt by Romani immigrants, but the cards were in Europe before the Romani (plus, the Romani came from Asia, not Africa).

Undeterred by the lack of anything approaching proof and despite the varying numbers of cards in different decks of the time, Gébelin further determined that the twenty-two Major Arcana cards were created to align with the twenty-two letters in the Hebrew and Egyptian alphabets. (Spoiler: Ancient Egyptians didn't use an alphabet; they had hieroglyphics.)

Regardless of his oversights and however unintentional, Gébelin's writing was incredibly influential with powerful people. By linking tarot imagery to Egyptian mysticism, the cards were deemed more credible. Tarot decks hadn't yet been standardized by this time—with the number and order of cards varying by creator and geography—until Gébelin revised the *Tarot de Marseille* deck to suit his theories regarding tarot's Egyptian origin as well as elements from Kabbalah.

Despite having no factual evidence of the existence of tarot cards prior to those used by Italian nobles, wealthy Europeans embraced Gébelin's explanations, and from that point forward, tarot shifted from leisurely pastime to esoteric mainstay. Although most of his theories have been debunked, Gébelin's work has had a lasting impact on tarot traditions.

A few years after Gébelin's writing hit the streets, Jean-Baptiste Alliette, a French occultist working under the pseudonym Etteilla (his name spelled backwards), published a fortune-telling manual titled *Etteilla, or A Way to Recreate Yourself with a Deck of Cards* in 1783. Like his predecessor Gébelin, Etteilla revised the meaning and etymology of the cards to align with his theories regarding tarot's Egyptian origins. After the European Renaissance, the influence of Kabbalah in non-Jewish culture soared as it was adapted to esoteric belief systems, and Etteilla further underscored the unproven relationship between Kabbalah and tarot.

Etteilla also added the natural elements and astrology to his interpretation of the cards in his five-part series titled *How to Relax with the Card Game Called Tarot*. In it, he outlined his approach to cartomancy and indelibly cemented tarot's link to ancient Egypt.

The first tarot deck designed specifically for divination is attributed to Etteilla, and it included Hebrew letters on the Major Arcana cards. While tarot has no historical connection to Kabbalah, Etteilla and his peers established one over time.

Completing the trifecta of French tarot trendsetters is Alphonse Louis Constant, a Kabbalah enthusiast who wrote under the name Éliphas Lévi, which was said to be an anagram of his name into Hebrew, but may have just been an attempt to seem more Jewish in an effort to legitimize his ties to Kabbalah.

In *Dogme et Rituel de la Haute Magie* (*The Doctrine and Ritual of High Magic*), published in 1854, Lévi fortified the correlation between tarot and Kabbalah, linking the Major Arcana as a road map to the

Tree of Life and spiritual enlightenment. Like his contemporaries, Lévi invoked ancient Egypt and Kabbalah to legitimize his tarot views with the authority of antiquity, and his revised meanings of tarot symbolism informed the most enduringly popular tarot deck of all time.

LONDON CALLING

The esoteric transformation of tarot culminated in Victorian England, where spiritualism was all the rage and séances were a house party must-have. The industrial revolution and scientific breakthroughs had displaced the supernatural mysteries of life in the late 1800s, leading to a renewed fascination with mysticism and spirituality. Tarot was widely available by this time as a tool for divination and self-discovery, and people created decks based on their own unique interpretations.

Interest in the occult was at an all-time high, and secret societies devoted to metaphysical studies started popping up in London. Today, these eccentric gatherings of mystics, scholars, poets, and artists might be called an artist collective. Back then, they had more colorful handles like the Hermetic Order of the Golden Dawn, which boasted celebrity members including the poet William Butler Yeats, *Dracula* writer Bram Stoker, and Sir Arthur Conan Doyle of Sherlock Holmes fame.

Occultist A. E. Waite and artist Pamela Colman Smith were both Golden Dawn members when he commissioned her to illustrate the cards for the *Rider-Waite* tarot, published in 1909 and named for Waite himself and the publisher William Rider.

Known today as the *Rider-Waite-Smith* deck to give Colman Smith her due, this deck was radical for its time because the Minor Arcana cards featured human figures and objects in allegorical scenes. Rather than the clusters of wands, cups, swords, and coins of past decks, every card was given a singular identity. Placed together, the cards now told stories with pictures that offered visual clues, allowing the user to create a personal narrative.

Waite and Colman Smith were presumably inspired by the *Sola-Busca* deck, which had been created by an unknown artist in 1491 and was displayed at the British Museum just as Waite and Colman Smith were designing their deck in 1907. Prior to the publication of the *Rider-Waite-Smith* deck, the mysterious *Sola-Busca* was the first and only fully illustrated seventy-eight-card tarot deck in existence. The influence is undeniable, with nearly a dozen cards from both decks sharing exact imagery.

While the artwork of the *Rider-Waite-Smith* deck is relatively simple, it is brimming with symbolism that deviates from classic tarot iconography. The figures' clothing, accessories, facial expressions, and landscapes all carry elements that support the archetypal story of the hero's journey. Traditional Christian symbolism was diluted—for example, The Hierophant and High Priestess replaced the Pope and Papess—while other Golden Order doctrines were highlighted, such as Hermeticism, Kabbalah, Freemasonry, and the Greek mysteries.

This was the first mass market tarot deck, and Colman Smith received little recognition (or money) for her work. She was a complex nonconformist who was ahead of her time—it has been suggested that she was a queer woman of color and confirmed that she was a vocal supporter of the suffrage movement (Colman Smith incorporated the last names of both parents). She was also synaesthetic—experiencing one sense through another, like hearing a sound and seeing it as a color—often painting visions that came to her as she listened to music. Although she was influenced by French occultists and the *Sola-Busca*, Colman Smith's intuitively designed imagery imbues a creative signature that has become the tarot template for countless variations since it was published, yet it remains the most iconic deck of all.

FEELING GROOVY

Aleister Crowley, the self-proclaimed nemesis of A. E. Waite, was an infamous British occultist who was once dubbed the "wickedest man in the world" and kicked out of Italy by Mussolini (you know it's bad when . . .). He was a member of the Hermetic Order of the Golden Dawn until being ostracized (Yeats *hated* him), and then decided to start his own religion, Thelema. He based it on his 1904 publication, *The Book of Law*, which he claimed had been dictated to him in Cairo (again with Egypt!) by an entity named Aiwass.

In 1944, Crowley teamed up with artist Lady Frieda Harris to produce the *Thoth* tarot deck and corresponding *The Book of Thoth* (taking Gébelin's cultural co-opting of ancient Greek texts one step further). Although still informed by the French style of the eighteenth century that lacked human figures, the abstract symbolism of the *Thoth* deck was a striking departure. It took tarot cards in a new direction with a kaleidoscope of styles, colors, and backgrounds conveying the meaning of each card.

Crowley's deck was not well received and likely would have faded into obscurity if not for the Beatles featuring him as one of the faces on the cover of their 1967 album *Sgt. Pepper's Lonely Hearts Club Band*. The 1970s saw many seeking personal transformation through alternative forms of spirituality that focused on harmony and expansion of consciousness. Whether through psychedelics, crystals, meditation, or tarot, people were searching for alternative tools and, twenty years after his death, Crowley transformed from occultist to cult figure. He became a pop-culture icon, and tarot was introduced to a generation eager to embrace his teachings as New Age practices.

TAROT TODAY

The evolution of tarot continues today. The cards have become a mainstream tool for self-discovery and healing used by therapists and witches alike. With movements centered on racial justice, gender equality, LGBTQ+ rights, and other special interests, tarot has been reimagined and modified to align with different groups and express new identities.

Lived experience and spiritual perspective are reflected in today's decks just as they were hundreds of years ago. Whether for the parlor games of bored aristocrats, séance holders in Queen Victoria's court, or the yoga teacher next door, the meaning of the cards has been refined over time, shaped by each era's culture and the needs of individual users.

Tarot cards were likely reinvented many times throughout history, from Asia and Africa to Turkey and Italy. I'm sorry if this bursts your tarot-is-from-ancient-Egyptian-tombs bubble, but how tarot found its way to you was never the point. Tarot may not have a sexy hieroglyphic origin story, and for me this further validates that tarot is what you make of it. How you use these cards is in no way dependent on the magical musings of Egyptian high priests. *Your* interpretation of the card is where you find the magic of tarot.

Tarot evolves on a macro level alongside art and culture, but it's also meant to change on a micro level as you develop as a person. If tarot can help you uncover universal truths and enhance your understanding of the world and how you experience it, then everything leading up to that discovery is irrelevant, including the history of the cards themselves.

The mystical beginnings of tarot may have been concocted by occultists, but that doesn't diminish the divinatory potential of the cards. If this seems too fantastical, consider that looking at pieces of paper with symbolic imagery for guidance isn't that different from the peculiar art, curious objects, bejeweled skeletons, levitating saints, and weeping statues found in religion today. Ancient faiths are crammed with oddities and inconsistencies that many accept at face value. And if the cards provide comfort, validation, and guidance to people regardless of their gender, race, or sexuality, isn't that powerful enough? The goal of many things metaphysical is to help you understand yourself on this journey called life; the tools you work with are secondary to how you work with them.

Tarot was never meant to be a strict dogma—since its inception, the cards have been altered to suit the owner of the deck. Don't be afraid to make tarot your own and let it develop to suit your style of reading; this is what practitioners have been doing for centuries. You're simply carrying on the tradition.

The genesis of your deck doesn't matter as much as the relationship you forge with it and how the unique message of each card applies to you in a relevant way. I may scoff at the way old white dudes doing tarot in eighteenth-century France connected it all to ancient Egypt and Kabbalah, but I'm not that different from them—instead of ascribing meaning to ancient cultures, I see connections to the work of Brené Brown and Esther Perel. Tarot meets you where you are and holds up a mirror to deliver wisdom in ways that resonate.

Tarot's roundabout lineage reveals constant reinterpretations and adaptations into the reader's worldview to help make sense of that particular world. And it will continue to adapt for you.

CHAPTER 2

∞

Woo Woo Without the Cuckoo
(How Tarot Works)

Here's the secret to reading tarot cards: Anyone can do it. All you really need is a deck with Major and Minor Arcana (more about choosing a deck in Chapter 3), your imagination, and some form of note-taking. You don't have to be an expert, and you definitely don't need to spend years memorizing the definition of every card.

Tarot tells you there's a place for you in this world by reflecting your world back to you. It's a tool for uncovering your natural gifts and talents as well as challenges and limitations. Tarot readings are a jumping-off point to understanding what's currently happening as well as what's waiting for you. Tarot doesn't carry the same judgement the rest of the world does; each card offers positives or negatives (sometimes both). There is no assigning of blame—only observations and considerations that are offered in a matter-of-fact, impartial manner.

A tarot reading will validate your dreams and show you how to achieve them by inviting you to take responsibility for your one precious life. You want to be empowered and enlightened to make the right decisions for yourself, rather than abdicating responsibility for your life to pieces of paper. Otherwise, the message of a card can become a self-fulfilling prophecy. Tarot calls on you to embrace your purpose and step into your potential. It's an energetic aid to your personal development.

The Tarot 101 definitions are an obvious starting point when learning the cards, and we'll cover them in Chapters 9–13, but my approach drills beneath the traditional message to look at deeper opportunities for growth, healing, and living your best life. You'll also learn how the meanings of the cards can deepen as the relationship between you and your deck develops over time.

Tarot cards can be used for self-exploration, and the way you interpret their messages is going to be formed by who you are, what you believe, and why you're using tarot in the first place. Their meanings are already made for you and ready to evolve alongside you—that's the magic of tarot.

SPIRITUAL HOTLINE (CONNECTING TO THE DIVINE)

Pretty much every life lesson, challenge, or opportunity can be highlighted, guided, or informed through tarot. But these aren't predictions—they're soul messages.

We're in a time of spiritual awakening that was amplified for many by the COVID-19 pandemic. People are questioning the status quo and reevaluating their priorities, seeking new ways to experience the world and their lives. This shift in consciousness is a transformative process that requires the shedding of old ways while having faith in an unproven and unknowable future, which is incredibly liberating—and also scary AF.

We're now realizing that intellectual rigor can coexist with the metaphysical—and there are multiple paths to the truth. It's why so many people are turning (some might say returning) to the ancient wisdom of mystical modalities like astrology or tarot, despite having access to unprecedented technological and scientific advancements.

Pulling a few cards can support your decision-making about everything from career and family to discovering your purpose. A reading can highlight what's blocking you from reaching your potential; help you recognize patterns so you can find healthy love; or detect and demolish lifelong insecurities, fears, and self-doubt.

There's a deeply human need for a greater connection to ourselves and to the unknown, and tarot offers a link to both. The cards help you understand your Divine path—what you have to offer and what you need to work on—in a way that is both extraordinarily practical and highly spiritual. The cards offer a glimpse of your celestial DNA, and their messages can put you on a path to your purpose, teaching you how to love and accept yourself along the way.

Tarot imagery encompasses ordinary life experiences and broader concepts of universal truth, providing spiritual clarity free from religious doctrine. When you consider the story or symbolism of a card, the way you relate to it can offer new insights and fresh perspectives, expanding your understanding of the world while anchoring your place in it. Tarot connects us to the mysteries of life, whether that's through cosmic intelligence, our own higher wisdom, or a combination of the two.

In times of tragedy, we need help processing the pain. We look for meaning and grounding when we're swimming in uncertainty. Tarot cards can give context to our suffering and help us navigate through it, while also reassuring us that this too shall pass. The cards inspire us as well, offering a sneak peek at the bountiful energies that are available to be leveraged if and when we're ready.

COUNSELING FROM THE CARDS
(TAROT AS A THERAPEUTIC TOOL)

Similar to journaling, exercise, or traditional talk therapy, tarot can support your emotional health by providing unbiased direction and alternative points of view. Through the symbolism of a card, you can gain insight into yourself. Like therapy, tarot is a powerful tool for reflecting on your inner and outer world, and we'll get into the specifics of how tarot can be used for self-help in Chapter 5.

MYSTICAL MYTH-BUSTING
(WHAT TAROT IS . . . AND ISN'T)

Tarot isn't fortune-telling. There are no messages of doom or foretold prophecies. A tarot reading doesn't give predictions—it offers agency. Tarot validates where you are, shows where you've been, and indicates what's possible. Each of the seventy-eight cards tells a different story, and together they can work to help you define a desired outcome, explore current energies surrounding you, or understand potential consequences of following a path. Tarot is like your longtime bestie, a trusted therapist, and a wise aunt who's seen some shit.

And while some cards are more fun or sexy than others, there are no "bad" cards—just bad tarot card readers. Even the most challenging cards can provide hope, guidance, or alternatives . . . and good tarot readers know this. Certain cards may look threatening, but none of them can hurt you. What they will do is inform you.

A tarot reading is a peek behind the curtain to see what's going on energetically so you can make the best decisions for yourself moving forward.

Instead of foreshadowing your future, tarot grounds you in the present. There's nothing mystical (and definitely nothing evil) about these pretty pieces of paper—tarot simply holds up a mirror to help you move forward with confidence.

THE DEATH CARD IS . . . GREAT? (WHY "BAD" CARDS ARE SO GOOD)

Tarot often gets a bad rap—some of it deserved because nasty people take advantage of the vulnerable—but there's nothing scary about it. For instance, I love getting the Death card because it's about transformational change. It's how you deal with change that can make it uncomfortable.

We can't shy away from the harder lessons that tarot teaches us, but we don't need to be afraid of them or dwell on the negative. The cards always provide information to help us navigate tough times. Although you may find yourself in tears during a reading, it's usually the result of a deeply resonating message versus me telling you that your cat's days are numbered—which, spoiler alert, the cards would never say and I would never do.

A well-known metaphysical shop in my town had a tarot card reader who was notorious for making dire predictions and wielding the Death card like a paper boogeyman. This approach traumatized her unlucky customers and reinforced every negative stereotype about tarot, leaving her clients to tiptoe through life convinced that a horrible fate awaited them. Not only was this tarot reader unethical (more on ethics in Chapter 7), but she was also dangerous because she promoted the fallacy that we have no agency in our lives.

The cards never tell you what's going to happen—tarot doesn't do predictions. During a reading, I would never give you winning lottery numbers or the name of your supposed soulmate. If you encounter a so-called psychic making bold predictions ("You'll be married by August!") or suggesting that you need to be cleared of negative energy—for an additional fee, of course—my advice is to get the hell outta there because you're dealing with a con artist. I'm not saying people like that aren't intuitive (although a busted clock is right twice a day), but they're also probably scamming you.

With tarot, intention is everything. If someone is determined to access threatening energy using tarot, the cards will deliver because they're a tool. I can pick up a hammer and use it to build a bookcase or smash a window—it's still just a hammer that I decide to use in a specific way. My intention with every reading I do is to help you unlock the wisdom that lies within you.

JUNG & TAROT: A LOVE STORY
(THE IMPORTANCE OF ARCHETYPES)

To learn tarot, it really helps to understand the ideas of Swiss psychoanalyst Carl Jung about the collective unconscious and archetypes.

The collective unconscious is like a shared database or cloud of cognition we're all born with, and it contains universal concepts we just seem to know (without knowing how we know them) called archetypes.

We instinctively make sense of the world through archetypes, and they often show up as characters in our myths and stories. We may be on very different paths, live in different countries or cultures, and have opposing points of view, but we all yearn for a mother's love, seek mentors for guidance, and look for help from heroes.

Our psyche is filled with archetypal images that structure how we understand the world, and they're often revealed in our dreams, giving us insight into our lives. Archetype examples include the hero, the mother, and the rebel. From ancient scriptures (Mother Mary) to modern gossip (the Kardashians), archetypes tell the story of humankind across civilizations.

Jung's work and tarot are both rooted in archetypes. Tarot is a universal vocabulary that uses the symbols and stories of archetypes (like The Fool or The Hermit) to speak the language of the collective unconscious. In a tarot reading, your story is told through archetypes, and they're familiar to you because they *are* you. These archetypes exist in the energetic blueprint of every person.

My clients live around the world—from Africa to Australia—and around the corner, and they're from all walks of life. It doesn't matter if I'm reading a celebrity in New York or a truck driver in Newfoundland: The cards always resonate because these lessons and stories have been reflecting our lives for centuries.

Every tarot reading, even a single card, has a unique message that we all interpret differently because it taps into the remnants of our shared ancestral experiences and applies this insight to our individual lives. I do a "Card of the Day" every weekday morning on Instagram, and half the time I wonder why I even bother because it's so obvious that the card's message is just for me. Then I get people contacting me all day telling me how that card spoke directly to them and was exactly what they needed to hear.

While the collective unconscious is reflected by tarot symbolically, these archetypes are at the same time very pliable. For instance, the Ten of Cups is traditionally about family, but for me it's about connections, since family comes in many forms. And the Nine of Coins is good money, but in my readings she exemplifies the Divine Feminine. I use modern examples to illustrate these modified meanings, making them relatable to my clients. Using the Ten of Cups as an example, I point out how good it makes us feel to help a friend who reaches out for advice, so we can give others that gift by letting them do the same for us because it makes everyone feel good. The best tarot readers explain the meaning of a card in ways that are based on their own perspectives and lived experience. By getting personal, you tap into something powerful.

Stories are medicine, and the symbols and patterns found in archetypes provide a framework for healing and expansion. In that sense, the stories of tarot are maps that guide you back to your innate knowing. The creators of the cards didn't come up with anything new—they tapped into something ancient. This is why the meanings continue to resonate today.

PRIVATE PARTS & PEDIGREE
(GENDER & RACE IN TAROT)

How can you reflect on life lessons and gain a stronger understanding of self through archetypes when the mirror you're looking in is overflowing with a bunch of old hetero white dudes? Tarot imagery has traditionally been grounded in an exclusively white, cis, colonial, and patriarchal point of view because that was its intended audience. Thankfully, the traditional composition of the cards is starting to change with the times.

I believe we all have an obligation to consciously create more inclusive spaces—featuring voices and viewpoints that have been underrepresented or ignored—and that includes tarot. This has been a journey for me over three decades, especially in terms of the Kings and Queens found in the Minor Arcana. These cards always stand for real people in my readings, and for a long time (too long), Kings were male and Queens were female. Period.

As I've evolved as a person, so has my interpretation of these cards. When a King or Queen shows up in a reading today, I explain that it's about characteristics rather than gender. All of us embody traits considered masculine and feminine to varying degrees, and the same is true in the tradition of tarot. The Kings and Queens represent particular characteristics that can tie into the archetypes of masculine and feminine, but they are relatable to anyone regardless of gender. Gender is fluid, and tarot can be too.

Whether in the ways you approach readings or the visual representation of the deck you use, all people should be able to see their lived experience reflected back at them. Whichever deck you choose (more on that in Chapter 3), make sure you're comfortable with the imagery and messages being conveyed.

ANY WAY YOU WANT IT, THAT'S THE WAY YOU READ IT

Regardless of what you read in this (or any other) tarot book, you'll want to develop your own opinions and interpretations. At its core, tarot is a way for us to contextualize our experiences. It's a tool to self-reflect and reclaim agency over our lives. It's not about letting the cards make decisions for us or tell us which paths to choose—it's about honoring our multitudes, as illustrated by the stories of the cards. There are endless depths to explore. We're not at the whim of these pretty pieces of paper, but if we pay attention, we can witness them reflecting our complexities back to us.

We'll get into the relationship between tarot, numerology, and astrology, but you can also delve into other esoteric components, like Kabbalah, if they pique your interest. Just keep in mind that tarot is like a bubbling pot of soup—you can sprinkle in other ingredients, but the base is still soup. The additional inclusions simply enhance the flavor in a way that appeals to you.

On this existential adventure called life, let tarot be your map, keeping in mind that how you work with this guidance is up to you. Instead of fortune-telling, a tarot reading often validates what you already know, shifts your perspective, and motivates you to take action—from baby steps to big leaps. Tarot is a teacher and a tool—what you choose to do with this information is always up to you.

CHAPTER 3

∞

Hit the Deck

(How to Choose & Care for Your Cards)

Are you ready to buy a tarot deck but overwhelmed by all the options? Do you already have a pack of cards that's gathering dust because you have no clue where to start? Or do you just want to spice up your relationship with your ride-or-die deck? Maybe you were given a deck and never opened it because it's covered in unicorns, and you hate unicorns.

Just like finding a life partner or picking the perfect melon, choosing the right deck is a matter of personal preference, past experience, and overall instinct. What resonates deeply for one person may elicit a shrug from someone else. There are so many factors at play—color, theme, size, and tradition are just a few—and it's crucial that you do your homework so you don't come home with a Delphic dud.

TRUST YOUR PICKER (CHOOSING A DECK)

Every reading you do is held in your deck, so it's important that you take your time determining the best one for you. The good news is, when it comes to tarot, there are thousands of decks to choose from. This is also the bad news because having so many options can be overwhelming when you're not sure what to look for in a deck, especially if you're new to tarot. But don't worry, I've covered a few of the essentials.

What's the Big Diff? (Oracle versus Tarot)

First things first: Make sure you're actually buying a tarot deck and not oracle cards. Just like tarot, oracle cards can be a tool for guidance and reflection, and both decks can have a specific aesthetic theme, but that's usually where the similarities end.

Chapter 8 has a deep dive on the anatomy of a tarot deck, but here's the core configuration: Tarot is made up of seventy-eight cards that are split into the Major Arcana and the Minor Arcana. The Minor Arcana has four suits (typically Wands, Cups, Swords, and Pentacles) numbered one to ten, as well as court cards (Page, Knight, Queen, and King). We'll get into themes and variations later, but this is the structure that has been used for hundreds of years.

An oracle deck has no rules—the number of cards and messaging behind them are only limited by the designer's creativity. Oracle cards can be a great introduction to cartomancy because each distinct (and sometimes lengthy) missive is usually written directly on the card so there's no need to learn the meaning; you can just read it. A single card can offer insight around one aspect of your life, a daily affirmation, or a concept to focus on, but putting oracle cards together in a reading can be tricky.

The efficacy of oracle cards can be hit or miss because card meanings are entirely dependent on the designer, while tarot is rooted in specific systems that still leave room for adapting and expanding. Compared to tarot, oracle cards have written explanations that may appear much easier to work with, and in some ways that's true. But tarot isn't intimidating once you realize that you aren't memorizing a bunch of definitions—you're learning stories. If you prefer oracle over tarot, or you rely on both depending on your mood or situation, that's great. I personally find that tarot cards offer more depth to a reading (otherwise I'd be known as Oracle Lori).

Cut from a Different Thoth (Lineage Variations)

Even within tarot, different traditions can alter the order of the cards and their meanings. The *Rider-Waite-Smith* system is the most commonly used today, with stories told through illustrations.

The *Marseille* tradition originated in France (as covered in Chapter 1) and predates the *Rider-Waite-Smith* deck by over one hundred years. The Minor Arcana of these cards look like a modern deck of cards (i.e., the Seven of Cups is just seven chalices without any story depicted), making it more difficult for beginners to grasp.

The *Thoth* tradition was created decades after *Rider-Waite-Smith* and relies on richly symbolic graphics to fuse a mélange of esoteric and metaphysical ideas into the cards. *Thoth* encourages users to imbue their own interpretations into the dramatic imagery, adding a layer of complexity that you may find inspiring or discouraging.

Watch Your Tone (Look & Feel)

Tarot is a visual tool, and through the imagery of the cards, you'll find symbols that relay the story. It's important to connect with the artwork from an aesthetic perspective. Are you drawn to sleek modern lines or cozy vintage vibes? Do you prefer soft pastels, simple neutrals, or bold splashes of color? Think about the style elements that appeal to you.

For many people it's also vital to work with a deck that reflects the world around them. Traditional tarot interpretations and imagery are rooted in patriarchy, so you can look for themes and visuals that resonate with you as a person instead. For example, there are many decks that present the messages of tarot through a BIPOC or queer lens.

Sometimes, it's simply a matter of what floats your boat. If you're an avid gardener, you can enhance the messages of tarot with a botanically based deck. Are you beguiled by dragons? There are dozens of options. Look for imagery that tantalizes your senses and messaging that speaks to your soul. Some cards will call you in ways you can't explain. If you're drawn to a deck and feel compelled to learn about it, or you just want to hold it while gazing at the images, that is more than enough reason to make it yours. Allow yourself to be seduced by the deck that's meant for you.

With so many modern decks inspired by the *Rider-Waite-Smith* version, it can be helpful to start with this one. Familiarizing yourself with this deck facilitates fluency in others. I learned to read tarot with a *Rider-Waite-Smith* deck, and I'm still using it thirty-five years later.

Get Handsy (How and Where to Shop)

When it's time to make your purchase, you may want to do some online research beforehand to see if any decks stand out to you (or you can dive right in and add to cart).

If possible, try to support local sellers. Visit a metaphysical shop or bookstore near you so you can handle their sample decks.

Any place that sells crystals will have tarot. Cards come in different sizes and weights; don't be shy to pick them up and spend some time with them. How do the proportions feel in your hands? Try shuffling the deck and drawing a couple of cards. Are they easy to maneuver?

If you're looking online, note the measurements and grab a ruler to gauge their size because you'll be shuffling and handling the cards while studying the images. Some decks are so tiny you could fit three of them in the palm of your hand, while others are as big as an iPad—when it comes to tarot decks, size matters.

Vibe Check (Tune In to Your Intuition)

No matter where you buy your deck, the most important thing to pay attention to is how it makes you feel. I've held decks and been completely turned off for reasons I couldn't articulate. Other times, I felt an instant familiarity that couldn't be explained, like the immediate connection you can feel with someone you've just met.

Whether you're shopping in person or online, notice your reaction to the cards—how do they make you feel in your body? Are you intrigued or nervous? Repulsed or enchanted? In love or indifferent? What energy are you picking up from the deck? Trust your first impressions, and if you're still having trouble choosing, ask yourself the following questions: Does this artwork (colors, patterns, styling) resonate with me? Is this deck based on a system (e.g., *Thoth*) that I understand or that I'm excited to learn? Do these cards give me a sense of their meaning based on an initial glance?

You can even grab your journal and write these questions at the top of the page, then take a moment to ground yourself with some breath before writing the answers (don't think about it—just write). It's like a pros-and-cons list with a sprinkle of intuition.

How Many Is Too Many?

When it comes to tarot, I'm extremely monogamous—I've had the same deck since day one, and it's been one of the longest and most fulfilling relationships of my life. Some people prefer an assortment of decks to choose from, depending on the person they're reading or the spread they're using. Others, like me, have one deck that is their ride-or-die.

Don't feel obligated to work with a single tarot deck or tradition. You may find that different decks speak to you as you gain skill and experience. Some tarot practitioners combine different decks for one reading or let their clients intuitively choose from an assortment. You could have a specific deck for your personal use and a separate one for reading others. If you're just starting to work with tarot, I suggest sticking to one deck and then expanding your collection once you're comfortable with the basics.

Gifted or Cursed? (The Purchasing Process)

A common myth is that your first tarot deck must be a gift. I think that's bullshit. You want your cards to resonate with you and that can be hard to figure out when you're not given a choice, but if you do receive a deck as a gift, or you really want your first one to be given to you, that works too!

A lot of people hesitate before buying a tarot deck secondhand, and honestly, I'm one of them. If you do get a pre-loved deck, be sure to cleanse the old energies so you can attune to it (kind of like getting rid of your ex's crap before the new love interest comes over).

I got my first deck way before Amazon (or the internet) existed, and I'd heard that it wouldn't work—or worse, would have bad mojo—unless it was gifted to me. In the 80s, one store in Calgary sold cards and crystals, so I dragged my friend down there and pointed to the one I wanted. She paid for my deck and immediately handed it over to me, and I took her to dinner to pay her back. My witchy mentor Erica later assured me that this was completely unnecessary. (Reader, she legit cackled when I told her.)

The diverse dialects found within the language of tarot can be overwhelming, so focus on one deck in the beginning, and if you find that it's not working for you, don't hesitate to put it aside and try something else. When you work with a deck that resonates with you, you'll start to establish a shorthand, and before you know it, you'll be fluent.

TAROT TLC (TENDING TO YOUR CARDS)

I was doing tarot at an event last week when a drink was accidentally spilled on my cards. The person just stared, frozen in mortification, as I calmly grabbed my cards and started drying them on my pant leg until someone brought some napkins. This wasn't the first (or even fiftieth) time my cards have gotten a little too close to the action at parties, so I was confident they'd be okay. But I wasn't always so easygoing with my deck. I've learned over time how resilient these pieces of paper can be. While fire and water are obvious threats, Cheeto dust can also do some damage if you let it. Whether card wear comes from physical use or energetic buildup, it's imperative that you clean and protect your deck.

KEEPING THEM CLEAN

My cards look their age—the images and words are faded, they feel worn, and they can be sticky to shuffle when it's humid. I personally love how my deck reflects the thousands of readings contained within it. These cards show a lot of wear and tear (just like their owner), and I've never been particularly precious in how I cleanse or store them, but that doesn't mean I don't treat them with reverence.

Kind of like detailing your car, you can go over each card and gently clean it with a soft cloth as needed (I use the same kind of cloth that cleans my glasses). Some people recommend furniture or baby wipes, but applying any kind of chemical to paper cards—even if it's safe enough for a baby's tush—makes me nervous. If spills or smudges occur, wipe the cards to dry them as best you can, and leave them to air out overnight. In thirty-five years, I have *never* physically cleaned every single card, but I do practice energetic upkeep. The easiest way to do that is through a ritual. If you're interested in rituals and want a deep dive, that's the subject of my first book, *Burn Your Sh*t: The Life-Changing Magic of Rituals*. Here are some of my faves you can use with your cards.

Smudge

The burning of herbs has long been associated with purging and purification rituals. Sage, palo santo, cedar, and lavender are popular choices for smudging. You can use a shell or any other fireproof container, a feather or your hand, and a smudge stick or loose herbs. Whatever your preferred method for smudging, make sure your supplies are ethically sourced. Set an intention before you begin to cleanse your cards, yourself, and the space you're in. Pass your deck through the smoke, making sure to open windows for the smoke to escape. Ask the Creator, Universe, Divine, or whatever spiritual energy resonates with you to create a sacred space for your cards to be used for the highest healing and greatest good of all.

Sound

Singing bowls, bells, and drums have been used in ceremony for centuries to move energy and connect with the Divine. Studies have demonstrated the physical and emotional benefits of working with the vibrations of sound, but it impacts the energy of everything—including your cards. You can plop your deck right inside a singing bowl and go to town. Try getting your groove on, dancing with your cards in the kitchen. Or grab some bongos to drum while your deck absorbs the beat. The power of sound is undeniable, and even if you can't discern a difference in your deck, I guarantee that you'll feel better after.

Visualize

The power of the mind cannot be denied, and sharing a moment of mindfulness with your cards is a beautiful way to cleanse and align with your deck; it works wonders at any time but is particularly useful when you first bring a deck home.

Hold your deck in your hands, close your eyes, and ground yourself with three deep breaths into your belly. As your breath returns to a normal rhythm, visualize a giant eraser wiping away any superficial energy that doesn't belong there... see it disappear with each swipe of the eraser. Now imagine waves of energy rolling through your deck, taking with them any dense or negative vibes (like a cosmic car wash). When the heavy energy has been removed, imagine a brilliant light coming down from the sky and entering the top of your head, traveling through your body all the way to your hands. Allow this energy to envelop your cards—let them marinate in this charged, purifying glow. Take three deep, cleansing breaths to close your visualization, thinking the word "wisdom" as you inhale and "healing" on every exhale. If these words don't resonate, you can replace them with some that do.

Moon Bath

Before you go filling the tub, this isn't that kind of bath. We've been harnessing the power of the Moon for centuries, letting it influence our crops and inform our rituals. Lunar energy peaks during a Full Moon, making it a potent moment to cleanse your deck. Infuse your cards with moonbeams during the pinnacle of *La Luna*'s power by placing your tarot on a windowsill. Don't worry if you can't see the Moon directly—the energy is still reaching you and your deck. I would never leave my deck outside overnight, mainly because of unpredictable weather, but also to prevent critters from damaging or stealing (or peeing on) my precious cards. And the good news is that isn't necessary; a windowsill will do you and your cards well.

Crystals

Tarot and crystals go together like PB and J. You can keep your favorite stones near you during readings or even incorporate them into your spread. Some people surround their deck with crystals when it's not in use, like a sparkly sentry. If you're new to crystals, try clear quartz, amethyst, or selenite—they all have excellent cleansing properties. I have a chunk of smoky quartz that I'll sometimes place in the middle of a reading when the energy is heavy. I never plan to do this; it's just an intuitive nudge that I listen to when it shows up. You can add some mystical razzle-dazzle to your readings with some rose quartz for love, black obsidian for dealing with denser energy, or celestite for connecting with your guides.

Absolutely Nothing

Is any of the above critical, or even necessary, in the care of your cards? Nope. Reading tarot isn't dependent on when you last smudged your cards. But if you feel better after performing a ritual (or two!) with your deck, then you do you, Babe. If you're delving deep into divination, then the energetic hygiene of you and your cards is more important. Imagine a picture frame sitting on a table for years without being cleaned—it's still beautiful, but it probably isn't as clear as it could be. The right ritual can help clear the path to your intuition so you can connect with your cards.

For some people, the more rules, preparation, and specific circumstances they require to give a reading can make tarot more difficult. Your cards don't need a Moon bath, smudging, special cloth covering them, sacred box, or special incantations—unless any of these things make you feel good. Then by all means, go to town.

The only ritual I do consistently is knock on my deck between readings—it clears the mojo of the previous reading, like an energetic palate cleanser. This is what I was taught by Erica on day one, and I've done it every day since.

One thing to note is that, just like a fresh pair of jeans or your latest love interest, you need to break in your cards to get comfortable with them when you first bring them home. That fresh deck isn't as untouched as it seems—a lot of people handled it before it landed in your hands. Before you start pulling cards, take a moment to clear the energy of others and connect to your own using any of the methods above.

KEEPING THEM SAFE

It's important to consider not only *how* you'll store your cards but also *where*. Will you put them on an altar out in the open? Are you expecting to take them on the road when you travel? Do you have curious kids or inquisitive pets? Think about where they'll be kept and who will have access to help you determine the best choice (remember to check in with your intuition!). Here are some popular options that can be found on Etsy or at your local woo woo emporium.

Cloth

Unwrapping a deck that is swaddled in a beautiful piece of fabric can feel like opening the perfect present every time you do a reading. You can choose any textile that entices your senses, from an elegant silk to a rustic linen. Enveloping your deck in fabric adds a ritualistic element to your readings before you even start, and the material can also double as a reading cloth.

Bag

A drawstring pouch is super cute and acts as a little bed for your deck. Although organza bags can be used for your cards and crystals, they aren't as protective (not to mention luxurious) as velvet, satin, or even leather. You can purchase handcrafted tarot bags on Etsy with one-of-a-kind designs or personalized embroidery that reflect your personality.

Container

Tarot boxes are as beautiful as they are sturdy, often with intricately carved designs and space for multiple decks (you can even throw some crystals in there to keep your cards company). Some have a sliding lid while others open up like a treasure box, but they are always an impressive statement piece.

The main drawback is that a container can be too bulky to cart around with you, so if you do a lot of tarot on the go, use a tarot box as a home base and have a portable alternative as well. I was gifted a gorgeous box and never really connected with it, so it's now a fancy storage container (some might say altar) for my lipsticks.

Original Box

It may not look as sexy as a hand-carved Balinese box or swathe of raw silk, but the little cardboard box your cards came in will do the job just fine. It keeps your deck safe and is easy to take with you.

∞

Aside from protecting your cards from the elements or the contents of the rest of your bag, don't stress too much about how you're handling, cleaning, or storing them. I keep my cards in a cute little handwoven container I found at a street fair years ago, and I've had to fortify it because it's falling apart from use. Before that, they were wrapped in a polyester scarf I had lying around the house. And for *years* before that, my cards lived in the original cardboard box. I'll sometimes leave them on a windowsill during a Full Moon, but I usually don't bother (their current home acts as a portable altar and mini charging station). Whether you keep your cards on an altar or stash them in your underwear drawer until you need them, they'll still work.

Tarot cards don't perform magic, but they can be very magical. Getting them dirty or dog-eared doesn't harm or diminish their potency because the power and magic of the cards comes from how you work with them. There is no wrong way to store and cleanse your cards. Try different modes and methods to see what aligns with you energetically (i.e. feels good). The most important thing for cultivating communication with your deck is to start working with it.

CHAPTER 4

∞

Tarot Tinder

(Getting to Know Your Cards)

If you try to memorize the meaning of every card before cracking open your deck, you might never start (not to mention you'll miss out on the magic of allowing your cards to reveal themselves). The fastest way to connect with tarot is to start pulling cards; this is how you make sense of the stories and learn how they resonate with you.

Tarot invites interpretation. If you're someone who thinks in absolutes and craves certainty, this can be difficult because the cards are more speculative than definitive. Rather than giving you clear-cut answers, tarot invites you to explore what's possible and intuit the best next step for yourself—like a supportive mentor imparting wisdom when it's most needed.

That doesn't mean the cards won't tell you what to do; they can be super bossy (I'm looking at you, Ace of Swords), but these directives—*Stop being so clenchy! Get your head outta your ass! Have a nap!*—are what you need to hear in order to heal and grow.

As you build a personal relationship with your cards, their meanings will eventually transcend the standard definitions (aka

Tarot 101), and your deck will become a mirror that reflects you and your situation in a new light.

It helps to have a dedicated journal for tarot—whether a handwritten notebook or notes on your phone—to track not only your interpretations, but also your progress. Dedicate a couple of pages to each card so you can write about what a card means to you (including how that might differ from the standard definition), the ways that a card's message shows up in your life, and any other tarot musings that need to be expressed. Your journal serves as a security blanket while you get familiar with the cards. With enough practice, the cards will start speaking to you, and you'll develop your own dialogue. Until then, it's good to have a written frame of reference. Trust that your cards will bring the messages that are needed based on the meanings you've ascribed to them—this comes with practice, patience, and curiosity.

DATE YOUR DECK (LEARNING THE STORIES)

Every weekday morning, I record a "Card of the Day" (CotD) and put it on Instagram. I started doing it almost a decade ago for the friends and family who made up the majority of my forty-eight followers. I initially posted CotD to my Instagram stories because they disappeared after twenty-four hours (my early on-camera attempts were *rough*). I would record in the elementary-school parking lot after dropping off my daughter, wedging the camera into the steering wheel and contorting myself to fit into frame. I also filmed CotD (too) many times in the middle of Walmart while waiting for my winter tires to be changed at the adjacent Mr. Lube. (Fun fact: You can still watch those as a highlight on my Instagram and, as a bonus, witness my pandemic hair transformation when I looked like half of an Oreo cookie.)

Whether I'm celebrating Christmas, traveling the world, or down with the flu, I never miss CotD because people have come to expect it. This was confirmed when I accidentally posted on a Sunday a few months ago; my followers freaked out thinking that it was Monday and they were late for work. (The card was Knight of Wands, which encourages more fun and adventure, so maybe tarot was onto something.)

For me, CotD is an ongoing conversation with the collective as the cards flow together in a reading that never ends. I'll sometimes hesitate to post these one-card messages because they're obviously (in my mind) just for me. But every single day I have people reaching out to tell me how much the card relates to them—or that they pulled the same one—further illustrating how the life lessons of tarot connect us all. My daily card not only informs the masses; it also provides a free tutorial for tarot newbies and gives me personal guidance for the day. I don't usually do readings on myself because I'm getting one every day.

I invite you to start a conversation with your cards by pulling one for yourself every morning. Start by shuffling the deck as you focus on what you need to know today. Ask the question out loud if you feel the urge. Place the deck face down and use your nondominant hand to cut the deck however many times you want. By using your opposite hand, you're creating a shortcut to your intuition. Some people recommend cutting the deck into a specific number of piles, but there is no rule. I used to cut the deck in half and have since evolved into four piles. However you end up cutting the deck (if you cut it), reassemble it using one or both hands.

Before we start getting into the nitty-gritty of each card, note that I'll be referring to the *Rider-Waite-Smith* imagery throughout this book because a) it's the deck I use and b) it's been the template for so many others. But the deeper meanings of tarot apply across the board regardless of which deck you're using; your intuitive interpretation of the images is just as (if not more) important.

Pick any card and really take it in. Sit with it for a moment and notice your first impressions. What pops into your head regarding the imagery? Pay attention to how it makes you feel because that's your intuition whispering to you. Does the card remind you of anything? Do any symbols stand out? For example, do you find meaning in the distant Sun on the Death card, the blindfold featured on the Two and Eight of Swords, or the lantern held by The Hermit?

What about the people shown on the cards? Do you sense that they're happy or mournful, wistful or angry, strong or weak? What specific moment in their life are you peeking into? What do you think will happen next? What needs to occur to change unfavorable circumstances? Is there obvious action within the imagery, like The Tower, or is it a moment of stillness, such as the Nine of Cups?

Do the colors of a card feel exciting or tranquil, scary or reassuring, inspiring or depressing? Pay attention to how your body responds to what you see before you. Do you get a knot in your stomach or butterflies? Does your hand tingle or your heart flutter? See if you can fully embody the experience by sitting with the feelings the card brings up and allowing them to surface within you.

Do any of these cards remind you of a person or past experience? When you personalize a card by relating it to people or events in your life, the meaning is much easier to remember. During readings, I share several stories from my life with my clients, and most find it incredibly helpful to relate the meaning of a message to their own lives (more on this in Chapter 14).

If the card doesn't speak to you at all, that's okay—there are no wrong answers! Your impressions may change over time, either that day or over years with your deck. What's important is to acknowledge what the cards are telling you and how it's being conveyed (e.g., physical sensations versus vibes). Think of it like an improv exercise:

You've just entered the stage in the middle of a scene and your job is to quickly surmise what's happening so it makes sense to you.

Take a minute to journal about your card before consulting the little guidebook that came with your deck. Compare your reaction to the traditional meaning, noting any similarities or differences. Does the guidebook reinforce what you already picked up from the card or give you a different perspective to consider? If you're working with a more modern deck, don't get too caught up trying to make it fit with the symbolism of traditional tarot—have faith that those stories will reveal themselves. And if you don't agree at all with the Tarot 101 interpretation, that's totally fine; just note it in your journal.

After reflecting on your card, put it aside and go about your day. Then, before you go to bed that night, look at the card again and think about how the message—whether from your interpretation or the standard Tarot 101—showed up in your day. Did the card give a warning or heads-up that helped you avoid something unpleasant? Did you look at a person or situation differently because the card's message shifted your perspective? In what ways did the essence of your card appear in your day? Does a card that confused you in the morning totally resonate by the evening? Record all of this in your journal along with any other musings that arise.

By focusing on a single card every day, you're immersing yourself in its story and taking your understanding to the next level. You're also kick-starting a conversation between you and your intuition as you start to trust what comes to you with each card. This is why your interpretation is just as important as the standard definition (or my explanation). It's essential to get comfortable doing mini readings on yourself because you get instant feedback about how and why a card communicates with you the way it does. This connection is always available to you because it's a part of you. Your job is to recognize it, listen to it, and trust it.

DEALING WITH FIRST DATE JITTERS

If your deck is brand new, you may want to introduce yourself to each card one by one before doing daily readings. You could go cross-eyed trying to do this in a single sitting, so aim for one suit at a time or a certain number of cards at once. Just as you would with your CotD, spend some time with each card and consider your reaction to it before looking at the guidebook.

You can also flip quickly through the entire deck and sort them into three piles as you go based on your first impressions of their color, style, theme, story, etc. The first pile is love at first sight—don't question why you feel this instant attraction, just go with it. The second pile is "no thank you" for whatever reason (e.g., the imagery immediately scares or bores you). The third pile is neutral—you don't actively dislike these cards, but they're not captivating in any way. When you're done, look at each pile and observe any correlations between the cards, such as style, story, suit, and so on.

Journal about your findings and then consult the guidebook to see if there are themes connecting your preferences. You can do this every so often to check if your tastes shift over time. Certain cards have been nothing-burgers for me since day one, while others have slowly become favorites. If you prefer some cards over others, don't worry about bias in your readings. The cards will tell their stories regardless of how you feel about them. Having awareness around which ones resonate with (or repel) you can offer valuable insight about areas in your life that you need to work on.

Try not to focus on memorizing the cards. I always tell my workshop attendees that I couldn't describe most of the numbered Minor Arcana by name, especially the higher numbers. For example, if you ask me what the Seven of Swords looks like, I'd have no clue—and I've had this deck for thirty-five years! But if you show me that card? I can talk about it for hours. And if you put it together in a spread with a few more cards? Now we have a *very* interesting reading full of insight, validation, and next steps.

KEEPING THE SPARK ALIVE

Even seasoned readers can benefit from trying different exercises to connect with their cards. Here are some of my faves:

Suits

Group the Minor Arcana by suit and line the cards up numerically side by side, leaving out the court cards. Similar to The Fool's Journey through the Major Arcana (more on that in Chapter 8), can you detect the path of a suit as you move through from ace to ten? A clear example of this can be found in the Wands. The figure in the Two of Wands is holding a globe while trying to figure out his next move, and it calls for an intention or objective to be set. The Three of Wands shows the same person in a new outfit without the globe—because he's decided on a direction. There is a literal progression being illustrated, and these visual cues are helpful when you're learning and serve as a foundation to build upon with experience.

Notice how the distinct characteristics of each suit are expressed in different ways and if you're instinctively drawn to one over the other. When you become familiar with the overarching themes, astrology, and elements of a suit (more on this in Chapters 10–13), you'll be able to explore the deeper meaning of each individual card.

Numbers

You can also sort the Minor Arcana by number (e.g., the Four of Wands, Cups, Swords, and Coins) and look for similarities that emerge within each group. Are there clear themes, such as sorrow, or distinct differences? The fives are an obvious example because they all give off a downer vibe. Others are more subtle, like the sevens, which help you get what you want in very different and equally effective ways (e.g., being decisive versus rising above the bullshit). If numerology is your thing, you can also do a deep dive on the characteristics of a number and how they apply to the Minor Arcana (I do more of a shallow snorkel in Chapter 8).

Stories

I've attended the transformative Allow workshops of writer Jen Pastiloff, and she'll ask me to pull a card as a writing prompt for the participants because tarot is a perfect creative catalyst. I offer my interpretation of the card, and everyone has five minutes to write whatever comes to mind. I'm always amazed by the beautiful and completely unique prose that is created from a single card. You can do this for yourself using one card or an entire suit. In addition to strengthening the connection with your deck, this activity also hones your writing skills while boosting your intuition.

∞

Some of the above exercises can be done in a day, but attempting to master tarot in one sitting is overwhelming and unnecessary. Thirty-five years later, my interpretations are still evolving because they're a reflection of my journey through life. Allow yourself the opportunity to learn from every reading. Give yourself plenty of time to work with your deck at a realistic pace. Remember, the relationship you're cultivating with your cards is meant to be a lifelong love affair, not a one-night stand.

In addition to sparking your creativity, a tarot reading can prompt deep conversations with your soul and the energy of the Universe. Once I started trusting my interpretation of tarot, the quality of my readings shifted from basic card definitions into full-blown channeling. With enough practice, the cards will start speaking to you and you'll develop your own dialect. For years, I felt pressured to fit my style of reading into the stereotypical tarot tropes, but through practice and perseverance (and not taking myself too seriously), I eventually gained the confidence to read cards my way. Now I love my very specific approach to tarot, and what separates me from the typical tarot card reader is exactly what appeals to my clients. Much like in life, I know I'm not everyone's cup of tea... and that's okay. Whether it's through me or another tarot reader, an astrologer, or a psychologist, whatever path leads you to clarity, hope, and healing is all that matters.

The only wrong way to read tarot cards is to do it with bad intentions. There are no rules that *must* be followed, and anyone claiming otherwise is probably trying to sell you something. Do what works for you, and set aside what doesn't. Take classes, learn from different teachers, and give readings to as many people as possible—you'll soon start to understand and, most importantly, trust what the cards have to say.

CHAPTER 5

∞

Therapy in a Box
(Tarot as a Self-Help Tool)

People often get a tarot reading for the same reasons they see a therapist: anxiety and stress, dealing with grief, figuring out their purpose in life, big life transitions, and relationship issues.

Tarot cards have long been associated with psychological principles, and I know a few counselors who incorporate tarot into their practice. We all want to understand ourselves better, and tarot lends itself to psychological introspection and excavation.

The power of symbolism has been woven throughout modern psychology, with Carl Jung being credited for introducing tarot into the mix as a tool connecting people to the collective unconscious through archetypes. He suggested that the archetypes found in tarot represent fundamental types of people or situations embedded in the subconscious of every person (e.g., The Emperor as a patriarchal or father figure). The stories of these symbols reflect the full spectrum of the human experience—from the mystical to the mundane.

A SPA DAY FOR YOUR SOUL
(HOW TAROT EASES ANXIETY)

We often exist in a state of perpetual catastrophizing because there are so many catastrophes occurring in the world all at once. Climbing out of a stress spiral can be difficult when the panic hormone cortisol is coursing through your system—and that's where tarot can help.

Pulling a card during a stressful moment can put things in perspective, allowing us to look at our circumstances through a more objective lens. Seeing your hopes and fears laid out in pictures can make the scary, painful, or unknown a bit more simple, manageable, and benign.

Most people are afraid of ambiguity and the potential for disappointment or harm. But the way I read tarot never leaves someone in the lurch (*Oof. Here's The Tower—sucks to be you . . .*). Though a card may reflect how crappy things are in the moment, there's usually a "but" that offers some insight into navigating the tough times or reassurance that they won't last forever. Or I may pull an extra card to bring more clarity to a challenging one. For example, the Nine of Wands encourages you to keep going, and Queen of Coins reminds you that wisdom comes from experiences that can be difficult. Oftentimes, when you're going through a rough patch, it can be hugely validating for the cards to say *yep, this is brutal* with an added *and here's what can help you get through it*.

The universal stories of tarot invite you to identify your emotions or understand your actions, making them less overwhelming in the process. Seeing your challenges reflected back to you in an image can also be comforting. A card like the Three of Swords looks dismal, but its message reassures you that you can handle these temporary setbacks, and your feelings around them are understandable.

Tarot pulls you into the present, and being in the moment activates your parasympathetic nervous system, bringing you to a place of calm (like when you breathe deep into your belly). Taking the time to reflect on a tarot card is a beautiful moment of self-care because you're intentionally focusing inward. That dedication to yourself is a balm for your psyche.

In uncharted territory, tarot acts as a compass that guides you to consider different avenues or points of view, especially when you're not interested in hearing them. The cards will always tell you what you *need* to know, not necessarily what you *want* to know, and sometimes we all need those stark reminders. Every time I pull The Hanged Man I think, *Ugh, this again*, because it's asking for patience on my part, but then I remember, *Yep, this tracks*, because patience isn't really my thing.

Magic can be found in self-awareness. It's not surprising that, according to a 2017 study out of the Pew Research Center, our interest in mysticism and spirituality is on the rise. People are turning to crystals, rituals, and other esoteric interests more than ever. Although we often can't articulate exactly how or why they make us feel better, does it really matter if they're doing the job?

We don't know what we don't know, and tarot can't offer certainty, but it does help us navigate an uncertain world with a bit more clarity and empathy—for others and, more importantly, for ourselves.

MINDFULNESS MATTERS (TAROT TO STAY PRESENT)

The cards can't tell your future, but they can help you be more present. Cultivating mindfulness does more than address anxiety; in being more present, you feel more like an active participant in your life. A 2004 study at the University of Victoria suggests that tarot can be a therapeutic tool of self-reflection because it invites users to examine their thoughts, beliefs, emotions, and judgements.

A tarot reading—even if it's just one card—is an invitation to better understand yourself, process tricky emotions, and consider next steps. You can pick a card to be a journal prompt, open or close a ritual, or simply sit with as you meditate on how it's impacting you.

Connecting with the cards helps you discover your story, but it's not a Magic 8 Ball. Your job is to work with the messages and determine how they apply to your life. Rituals are habits infused with loving intention, and tarot can be a part of that. Incorporating a daily card into your morning or evening rituals can help you set an intention at the start of your day or provide reflection at the end of it—or both! And if you find you want to build out your ritual practice beyond tarot, my first book, *Burn Your Sh*t: The Life-Changing Magic of Rituals*, has everything you need to get started.

TAROT-COLORED GLASSES (GET A FRESH PERSPECTIVE)

Tarot messages are neutral, free from political or religious dogma. They're also universal (because: archetypes). Your issues are externalized and mirrored back to you in a more objective format when viewed within the context of a card.

A tarot reading demystifies challenges that may have appeared massive so you can see them in a new light. The symbolism of tarot is ideal for creating a storyboard of your life in that moment; you're able to make a more informed decision from a place of clarity and calm when the visuals are laid out before you. Certain possibilities, situations, relationships, or situationships are reframed so you can view them more objectively.

Tarot cards bypass your head and heart to access your gut. You can see a card and instinctively know *exactly* how it applies to you. For example, if you're freaking out as you pack up your life to move across the country and pull the Ten of Cups, you can be reassured that family comes in many forms and you'll make connections wherever you go. It's also a reminder to lean on and leverage the current connections in your life when needed, which is often the last thing you want to do in these moments. Tarot is a mirror that allows you to see what may be obscured during trying times.

READER, HEAL THYSELF (CULTIVATING COMPASSION)

Self-love is one of the most important and challenging lessons that tarot teaches us. In healing ourselves, we heal others and the world. Tarot has no time for cocktail-party chitchat—it clears the superficial crap out of the way to get to the good stuff, opening the door to your spiritual evolution.

A tarot reading can disrupt unhelpful patterns and discard false narratives so you can make proactive changes from an empowered place. Instead of just looking at a card's meaning, consider what it means to you. How are you being guided to love yourself as you forgive others? What prevents you from living a life of abundance in all forms? Who told you that you weren't worthy (and why do you still believe it)?

Tarot cards make you feel seen and embolden you to act. They encourage contemplation that ignites what was dormant. You realize that your limitations are self-imposed because you learned long ago that asking for more was asking too much. In a reading, you recognize your truth.

Questions may be answered, but more often tarot simply validates what you already know deep down. The cards remind you that you're worthy—you always have been.

THE DOG ATE MY WOO WOO
(CONFIRMATION, CLARITY & ASS KICKING)

Tarot is the ultimate accountability partner. Some cards come with homework, and tarot will call you out if you ignore the assignment. Sometimes my regular clients will get repeating cards and sheepishly confess that *No, Tarot Lori, I did not read that book you recommended*, or *Nope, I haven't meditated once since I last saw you*.

I might assign a Full Moon fire ritual (Six of Cups) to help you pull some energetic weeds, followed by a manifesting exercise (Seven of Coins) to start planting new seeds. Or you'll be asked to learn the power of vulnerability from Brené Brown (Page of Cups) before visualizing the murder of your inner critic (The Devil). The Chariot signifies success that is being impeded by not moving forward, but I go upstream from there to point out the big choices that need to be made along the way. You can adopt this cosmic homework into your readings, create your own, or skip it altogether. Take what works for you and ditch the rest.

One of my best friends kept pulling the same few cards for *decades* until she initiated some major shifts in her life. After that, she started getting cards she'd never seen before. Like the proverbial horse to water, tarot can lead you to what's possible, but it can't force you to change. The cards merely help us bypass our conscious mind, which often acts like a grime-covered filter through which we view the world. If we ignore this newfound clarity, it won't go away just because we don't like what we see.

For example, if you're waffling between two job opportunities and you pull the Seven of Cups, you're being reminded that the key to making the right decision is to be decisive. I offer some intuition hacks to help you with this (see Chapter 6 for more). If you ignore what this card is telling you and keep wavering between offers, both may disappear.

The good news is that tarot's messages are always given in service of living our best lives. The bad news is that the action required on our part might feel scary or uncomfortable, even if the outcome is amazing.

∞

Tarot is flourishing hundreds of years after it came on the scene because it remains relevant to every generation in various applications. The cards have an uncanny ability to tap into universal concepts that resonate on a deeply personal level.

Delving into the meaning of a card opens your mind to new possibilities and provides validation that you're on the path to your purpose. It's also one of the most powerful tools for connecting to your intuition.

Although tarot is never a substitute for therapy, it can be the perfect complement for personal development. You can't replace prescribed medication with the cards, but you might consult your deck to identify the barriers or limiting beliefs keeping you stuck, or to explore the actions required to move forward.

CHAPTER 6

∞

Be Your Own Psychic
(Tarot & Intuition)

Intuition is the compass we all have when we're born that is often dismissed or suppressed by our caregivers, teachers, bosses, and partners. But we can also drown it out with our own insecurities, fears, and biases.

The word intuition literally means "to look within," and we're all equipped with the ability to answer questions big and small, but recognizing our inner voice so we can tap into that well of wisdom is tricky (and trusting it can seem impossible).

On the surface, intuition is hard to identify (let alone quantify) because it's inexplicable, intangible, and personal—but you can't deny that it exists or how powerful it can be. Who hasn't had an experience where listening to their inner knowing saved the day, or when disregarding it unfortunately blew up in their face?

Everyone is psychic. This ability may be amplified in some more than others, but it's there. Certain people are excellent at sports or music, and while I'll never score goals or play the piano, I can still kick a ball and carry a tune. We can all practice strengthening our intuition through a variety of methods, from meditation and journaling to working with crystals and runes. Tarot is simply one method.

The more you cultivate the little voice so often ignored, the easier it will be to take intentional steps toward your ideal future. By turning your gaze inward and balancing the connections between your intuition, intellect, and emotion, the better equipped you'll be to sit in your personal power and speak your truth.

Accessing your intuition gives you agency in life. You regain control over your sense of self and write your own narrative when you make decisions from an intuitive place. Listen to your inner knowing and watch it lead you to your highest healing, greatest good, and most bountiful outcomes.

TRUST YOUR GUT (SEPARATING EGO & INTUITION)

Culturally, the conscious mind has enjoyed a place of privilege for centuries, but science is now confirming that more often than not we're operating instinctively. And it's not just the metaphysical girlies who are leveraging intuition: In 2014, the United States Navy invested millions of dollars to help its sailors fine-tune their spidey senses, having seen how often intuition superseded intellect in high-pressure situations.

In addition to keeping you safe, accessing your intuition can transition you from a life of never-ending obstacles to one of ease and flow. But how do you discern between intuitive clarity and the internal fears, implicit prejudices, and unrealistic expectations that we all grapple with?

Start by paying more attention to what your body has to say because intuition transcends the conscious mind and sinks into the physical form. Scientists have nicknamed the gut the "second brain" because hidden within the gastrointestinal tract is the enteric nervous system—an incredibly complex network of over one hundred million neurons—which uses the same chemicals and cells as the main brain, not only aiding in digestion but also letting us know when something's not right.

According to the Center for Neurointestinal Health, bacteria in the gut and their by-products can affect our mood, cognition, and even behavior. And UCLA scientists were surprised to discover that 90 percent of the fibers in the vagus nerve—which regulates body functions such as digestion, heart rate, and immune system—convey information from the gut *to* the brain, not the other way around.

It turns out, it's often not your anxiety causing bloating and IBS—it's the other way around. Bodily sensations, like explosive diarrhea, are the second brain's way of alerting the main brain that shit is (literally) about to go down. Basically, your bowels are telling your brain how to feel about something, which can be helpful (though not always appreciated or convenient) when our main mind needs time to catch up. I haven't eaten mussels in over twenty years because food poisoning landed me in the ER the last time I tried them (Tarot Lori tip: Avoid seafood if you live in the Canadian prairies), but that's very different from the nonstop nausea I felt from the moment I accepted a job that ended up being a huge mistake. Sometimes your gut is dealing with gut stuff; other times it's pointing out what you've been ignoring, denying, or missing.

Both brains are in constant communication, sending messages to each other within milliseconds. And while your second brain can't do your taxes or write poetry, it can give you butterflies in your stomach or a sense of foreboding, which in turn informs your mood and makes you pay attention.

Your gut responds nearly instantaneously when something's

not right, acting as a primitive warning system. But the stakes aren't always so intense, and that's when your ego can get in the way. The ego is not concerned with your best interests; it feasts on shame and blame, criticism and conformity, and especially fear. The energy of fear is pushing, forcing, avoiding, and rejecting. There can also be constricting or minimizing sensations, such as panic or desperation.

Intuition appears quiet, calm, and grounded. It has an energy that confidently draws you in, guiding you toward the best choice even if, and sometimes especially, it's not the easy choice. Although it might not feel comfortable, intuition mixes a sense of excitement and anticipation with a certain knowing. By feeling into this energy, you follow your intuition.

Our intuition thrives in presence, so carve out time for stillness. Allow the quiet knowing to be felt and heard. Any form of intentional solitude will amplify your intuitive voice—you can meditate for an hour or walk around the block without your phone—intensity isn't as important as consistency. (Having said that, I haven't done either in two weeks as I edit this book and prepare for Christmas... we do the best we can with where we're at.)

Rituals are a great way to promote mindfulness and bolster your intuition. They minimize the worries that are weighing you down or impeding access to intuitive insight. The right ritual—even if it's just having a bath, holding a crystal, or sitting in nature—can raise your vibration, opening you up to the energy of the Divine and connecting you to a higher wisdom within.

While science is more comfortable with the biological aspects of intuition that can be measured, it's the connection to Spirit that catapults your intuition to new dimensions, leveraging unseen energy in the pursuit of your highest goals, deepest healing, and lasting peace. When we feel a (higher) power in our corner, it helps us trust our inner knowing. And this is where tarot can help.

PSYCHIC HOTLINE
(CONNECTING TO INTUITION WITH TAROT)

I believe that intuition is the language between Self and Spirit—and tarot is the vocabulary. A tarot reading is a conversation, not a sermon. The cards offer clues and validation, not commands or ultimatums.

Your deck isn't a crystal ball, but tarot can help you validate your intuition, releasing you from doubt and desperation to show you what is deeply true. It usually tells you what you already know but are resisting for some reason, such as a fear of failure (or success).

Although the cards can't learn your lessons for you, they can guide you along the way by reflecting an action that needs to be taken or awareness that is being willfully ignored. The mirrorlike magic of tarot invites you to discover what has been hidden or reconcile your past so you can move forward less encumbered.

If you choose to disregard what tarot tells you, life has a way of letting you know by other means, kind of like swapping the gentle tickle of a feather for a brick to the face. Paying attention to what we already know deep down can make the lessons we need to learn much less extreme.

Ideally, a reading will shed light, provide support, and instill confidence. The cards offer you agency and fortify self-worth, empowering you to make your own decisions and direct your own healing. Tarot is a conversation starter between you and your intuition, bridging the physical world and spiritual realm, and your job as a tarot reader is to pay attention to whatever comes up (physically or otherwise) because that's your intuition connecting you to a different kind of energy.

I'm very intentional with the words I use in my readings to describe each card, but that's just a jumping-off point. Depending on how the cards show up or what questions are asked, I share any thoughts, visuals, or physical sensations that may arise (which is why I keep a family-size bottle of Tums at my side during readings).

If a random image or word pops into your head when you pull a card, especially a card for someone else, make a note of it or tell the person. I've had the strangest visuals and vibes come to mind during readings. For years I wouldn't say anything out loud, but I finally trusted that it wasn't my imagination and started telling people—*that's* when the quality of my readings skyrocketed.

In every single reading I do, there comes a moment when someone says a variation of the following: "It's so wild that you're saying that because I was just listening to a podcast (or talking to my friend or reading a book) about this exact thing . . ." When you're thinking about a situation in a specific way and then I come along and reiterate your thoughts? That, dear reader, is solid woo woo.

The cards can let you know what you need to be aware of while also validating what you already know, or they might help you reflect in a new way on something that's already happened. A friend of mine recently led a retreat and asked me to pull a card for both her and the group before it started. She got The Tower (learning difficult but necessary lessons) and the Four of Swords (unplug to restore and strengthen your energetic core). We both assumed these cards were referring to the attendees' experience because they'd be doing lots of soul excavating with healing meditations. This was true, but it also applied to my friend, who got knocked on her ass with a brutal virus just as the retreat started. She was forced to surrender to her situation (not easy for her) and rest until she felt strong enough to continue. Thankfully, her co-facilitator, a yoga teacher, was able to pick up the reins, but my friend ended up learning a lot about herself that weekend, too.

Do you see how her cards gave guidance that was prescient on different levels? Not in a fortune-telling *You'll be barfing in a toilet for five hours this weekend* kind of way; it was more of a *Keep this in mind* message that helped her process the weekend from a more enlightened place. That's the beauty of tarot—it can be applied to different areas of life in different ways, and all of it can be true.

To help you connect with your intuition, I've provided a meditation that you can do before working with your cards or any time you're (intuitively!) compelled to do it. You can record yourself reading this meditation and listen to it or scan the QR code at the back of this book to access a recording of me leading you through it.

Awaken Your Third Eye (Intuition Meditation)

Find a comfortable position for your body, either sitting or lying down. Slowly settle into stillness, closing your eyes and drawing attention away from external surroundings or distractions as you focus on your breath. Notice how the breath flows in and out of your body with every inhale and exhale. Feel the gentle rise and fall of your chest and belly as you breathe. When your mind wanders, unplug from the mental chatter and come back to your breath, inhaling and exhaling as you drop fully into your body.

Notice any stress in your shoulders and let it go. Allow your shoulders to drop as you focus on your breath. Feel the muscles around your eyes relax. Bring awareness to any tension in your neck and jaw, and release it now. It's okay to let all this tension go as you soften into yourself. Let your tongue go heavy in your mouth. As you ease into a place of complete calm, your mouth may open slightly. Simply relax into this moment.

Bring your attention to the lower part of your belly, just below the navel, and place both hands there. Connect to this space with three deep, grounding breaths.

On your next exhale, expand your awareness to the space between your eyebrows and feel the energy growing. You may see an indigo-blue light spinning or feel a sense of expansion.

Focus once again on your belly and imagine an energetic line starting just below the navel that moves up the center of your body to connect with your third eye. Draw that energetic path from the inner knowing of your gut to your higher wisdom. Know that this connection is always available to you, ready to be accessed at any time. Let this intuitive path guide you to step into the flow of the Universe.

Now, imagine that you are going down a long set of stairs. Count them as you go down, down, down. You arrive at a door with a sign overhead that says *Intuition*. Beside the door is a table with a large key resting on top. Pick up the key and use it to open the door with ease, then walk through the door.

What do you see? How does it sound? Are you feeling a certain way? Allow yourself to explore this space.

Now hear any messages you are meant to receive.

After you have received all of your messages, and when you are ready, walk out the door. Place the key in your pocket, secure in the knowledge that you can access this space whenever you need guidance or simply want to return.

Close the door behind you and ascend the stairs. Return to your body and the external space you occupy. Slowly bring your attention to this moment and your surroundings. Take your time as you reawaken your body. Stretch into the space around you, wiggling your fingers and toes. When you're ready, open your eyes and smile.

Take some time to write about your experience and the wisdom you brought back with you. Moving forward, be mindful of the ways your intuition announces itself. Keep track of what happens when you listen to your inner knowing. Take note of the ways your intuition is always working with you, through you, and for you.

Your intuitive light is a flame that must be tended. For some it may shine a little brighter, but we can all bask in its glow. When you trust your intuition, you fortify your relationship with yourself. Anyone can build their intuitive muscles with enough practice and persistence, and tarot cards are the perfect partner to access the profound insights that often appear as whispers.

CHAPTER 7

∞

Don't Be a Dick
(The Ethics & Etiquette of Tarot)

Before we get too deep into the cards, it's worth going over dos and don'ts to ensure that you tarot responsibly. Some might consider "ethical tarot" to be an oxymoron because tarot readers are often associated with scammers, whether a sketchy street vendor or catfishing Instagrammer. But even if you're just pulling cards with friends, a code of conduct is critical when working with tarot. You owe it to yourself and the person you're reading to take tarot seriously, and an ethical code helps you do that.

It's like you're a cosmic hairdresser—a soul stylist, if you will. Your intention when working with cards can be beneficial (helping people feel their absolute best) or destructive (making things even worse). People often look to tarot when they're in a vulnerable place or stuck at a crossroads. They're putting their faith in what the cards say, even if it's just you and your bestie. Watch your words and be mindful of your methods because they matter.

Tarot reading isn't regulated, so it's up to the reader to keep things legit. A code of ethics protects you as well as your clients, even when it's your sister, helping you maintain boundaries during readings and ultimately making the experience better for everyone. Below are some things to consider as you develop your own tarot code of ethics.

THIS AIN'T 1-800-PSYCHIC
(PREDICTIONS VERSUS GUIDANCE)

I never claim to predict the future—I state the opposite very clearly before every reading. Tarot isn't about guarantees or prophecies. The cards offer a snapshot of the energetic landscape, giving my clients the nudge they need or validation they're seeking. But the answers ultimately come from the people themselves because they have free will. A mirror doesn't tell you what to do, but it can show you how things are.

But Tarot Lori, don't you consider yourself to be psychic? Absolutely—everyone is, including you. Some people have the volume cranked up a bit higher than others, but it's something that can be honed over time with practice, patience, and trust.

When I have an intuitive hit, the cards will often validate me (along with physical sensations like goose bumps or acid reflux). For example, someone will ask a question about quitting a job, and I'll have an immediate "yes" reaction before picking the Eight of Cups, which encourages leaving situations that are no longer in alignment.

You don't need your "clairs" (aka psychic abilities) cranked up to one hundred to read the guidance within the cards. Just stick to the story of a card in the beginning, and let your intuition develop along with your relationship to your deck. Keep in mind that no matter how skilled you become, it's always unethical to suggest that the message of a card is an absolute because that removes free will from the equation, and this disempowers the person you're reading.

Our lives, and the Universe we inhabit, are infinitely more complex than we'll ever know, so remove the pressure on yourself to provide predictions.

ZIP IT (CONFIDENTIALITY)

When people get a reading with me, they know I won't repeat what's said during our time together. This is partly because my short-term memory is the pits, and I forget readings five minutes after they end, but it's also *very* uncool to blab about other people's lives. It's usually implied, but you can assure people of confidentiality at the start of a reading to establish a safe space that encourages vulnerability and openness. And then stick to that promise—it's sacred.

MIND YOUR BUSINESS (THIRD-PERSON QUESTIONS)

This is a big one.

It's a common tarot trope that people get a reading to find out what (or if) their ex thinks about them, if a parent's health will improve, or if their daughter is getting married this year. Asking about another person is known as a "third-party reading," and it's an invasion of that person's privacy.

When you inquire about others without their permission, you're trespassing in their energy. And listen, I understand the appeal—isn't being psychic all about getting to know things that you couldn't otherwise know? Actually, no. Dipping into someone else's energy is like reading their mail or putting a peephole in their bedroom—it's creepy and intrusive.

A good (and ethical) tarot reading focuses on the person being read. Instead of asking about someone else's intentions, feelings, or actions, inquire about how you might be impacted by that other person. For example, "Will Sharon screw me over if we go into business together?" shifts to "What do I need to know about partnering with Sharon on that project?"

Rather than asking about someone else, ask what you need to know about that person within a certain context or situation. For example, "Will my mother's health improve?" becomes "How can I best support my mother right now?" Also keep in mind that when you ask about your relationship with an ex, cards will usually come up telling you it's time to move on. Focus on the person getting the reading, even if that's you, to get guidance you can work with. (Chapter 14 details how to frame questions for maximum impact.)

DON'T HOLD BACK (THE IMPORTANCE OF HONESTY)

By holding back the message of a card, even with the best intentions, you're doing the person you're reading a disservice. As I've already mentioned, there are no "bad" tarot cards—just bad tarot card readers. Some cards are more challenging than others, but you don't want to freak people out or deter them from taking action, because within challenges come opportunities for great insight and growth. If the person you're reading is struggling and heavier-looking cards appear (The Tower, The Devil, Eight of Cups, and Three of Swords are a few doozies), explain how these cards can be weirdly reassuring or validating. My readings never leave people twisting in the wind; there will always be some sort of guidance to help them navigate tricky times. The cards are meant to support us on our journey, not force us to take action. Let others make empowered decisions for themselves with all the information available to them from the cards.

Even the validation that "Yep, you're in the shit right now" can be exactly what someone needs to hear in order to keep going, along with the reminder that "This won't last forever . . . it just feels that way when you're in it."

YOU'RE NOT THEIR MOMMY
(BE A COACH, NOT A CAREGIVER)

I always say that my readings are a conversation with your soul and I'm the interpreter. Just as the cards are here only for guidance, the same goes for you as the tarot reader. Your job is to tell the story of the cards so your client (even if that's your bestie) can make informed decisions. Let the hard lessons land, but do it with kindness.

Also be mindful of people trying to use tarot as a crutch. I've had to gently talk some clients out of getting a reading because they just saw me a week earlier. They might be craving another tarot hit because the validation, reassurance, and support feels so good. But they also need to live their life—and do the homework they've inevitably been given. A reading is meant to cultivate empowerment, not dependence.

DON'T BE A JUDGE JUDY (COMPASSION IS KEY)

Nobody (even a psychic) really knows what someone else is going through, so try to leave your judgement at the door. Treat every person you read with empathy and respect. You're the messenger, not the adjudicator.

This can be easier said than done, especially when people make questionable choices or keep repeating the same dumbass mistakes. Remember, we've all done stupid stuff that leads to profound growth. Deliver the message and allow it to meet the receivers where they're at.

JUST SAY NO (TRICKY TOPICS TO AVOID)

Treating people with compassion doesn't mean you have to agree to every request. It's okay to refuse someone your services. I don't read children without parental consent, and for very young kids, it's usually just pulling a single card because a) their attention spans can't handle more than one and b) cards don't really resonate until adolescence. I'm not sure if it's because of early brain development or limited life experience, but the more complex lessons don't really land with younger kids. Being discerning about whom you read (and stating clearly how you can and cannot help them) applies to people of any age.

When necessary, I'll encourage clients to seek the help of lawyers, counselors, accountants, or doctors if I feel they need it, and I have a list of professionals I can refer them to (I don't get any kind of compensation for this—they're just people I know and trust).

People can ask me about their health and finances, and the cards will often have messages like *You need to meditate* or *Don't let things slip through the cracks*, but I always remind the client that none of the cards will tell them to check their cholesterol or buy a certain stock. Tarot doesn't deliver slam-dunk specifics. If it did, I'd be retired on my yacht in Saint-Tropez.

CURSES, CURES & OTHER CONS
(SCARE TACTICS & UPSELLING)

This one may seem obvious, but it's worth mentioning—more as a PSA for you as a person rather than a directive to you as a tarot reader: If you think there's a curse on you, or your house is possessed by spirits, I'm not your gal and tarot is not your answer. My other book (*Burn Your Sh*t: The Life-Changing Magic of Rituals*) has a whole chapter on cleansing your space from funky mojo, but evil energy is not in my wheelhouse, and I turn anyone away who is looking for such services.

Also, I think curses are bullshit. Can people direct negative thoughts or intentions your way? Of course. Can it ruin your life?

Only if you let it. There are a lot of damaged and desperate people in the world who will prey on the insecurities of others. I'm a firm believer in the power of positive *and* negative thinking; both can have a tremendous impact on your mental, physical, and spiritual well-being. If any so-called psychic tries to upsell you on additional paid services by implying you have negative mojo only they can remove, take your money and run.

I assign homework of some form in every reading I do, but it's always along the lines of "Have a bath and a nap" or "Burn Your Sh*t" rather than selling gimmicky products or pricey solutions.

WE DON'T NEED NO EDUCATION (CERTIFICATION REQUIREMENTS)

There is no officially recognized organization that licenses tarot readers, and you don't need to take any special classes to become excellent at it. Although many well-known tarot practitioners offer classes with a special certificate at the end, it's totally unnecessary. Just grab your deck and start pulling cards. As with anything, proficiency comes with practice. You can see my bona fides in my bio and be assured that I absolutely know what I'm doing without ever having paid for special accreditation. My work is constantly evolving, and my education is never-ending . . . it just comes from doing readings.

KEEP IT CLEAN (READING UNDER THE INFLUENCE)

This is a personal choice for everyone, but I will never do tarot if I've had anything to drink (and drugs have never really been my thing). Believe me, nobody wants a reading from Tarot Lori after she's had a couple of cocktails. It can be hard to remain as mindful of your words under the influence, and that can spell trouble when you're digging around in someone's energy. If you do decide to bring out your deck in that situation, keep the other ethics of tarot in mind and read responsibly.

MIND YOUR MANNERS (TAROT ETIQUETTE)

Certain courtesies should be kept in mind as both a tarot reader and client. Here are some basics; feel free to adapt or add to them as you see fit.

Be Honest

When you give a reading, don't sugarcoat challenging messages, but also be compassionate in how you communicate them. Interpret a card without directing the outcome—that is for the receiver to determine. Making empty promises and offering false comfort won't be helpful to anyone. Every problem has a solution, and your job is to empower the other person to discover it for themselves, with guidance from tarot.

Also, if someone asks about astrological implications or Kabbalah connections and you have no clue what they're talking about, admit it. I'm not really into numerology, so my knowledge is thin in this area, and every so often someone will ask me to go deeper about the significance of a card's number. I'll simply own it and suggest they do their own research into the meaning; this allows me to focus on what I *do* know.

This Is Not a Test

If you sense that the person you're reading is trying to trick or test your capabilities, shut that shit down with a simple phrase: "I'm getting a sense you're not really into this . . ." Then gauge their reaction to see if it's worth continuing. A tarot reading is not the time or place for guessing games, and it's a waste of everyone's time to have you prove your prowess. That is some Psychic Hotline nonsense. Tarot is a tool that I've used in a profoundly healing way on myself and others—I have no interest in convincing skeptics about its efficacy.

Hands Off

Always ask before touching another person's deck, and if someone starts groping your cards without your permission, inform them that an invitation is required to handle your energetic tools.

If you let people shuffle your cards, be clear about how you want them handled. Do you like the heads at the same end (like me)? Are you okay with the riffle shuffle used by blackjack dealers? Consider if and how people can touch your deck and make sure you communicate your preferences clearly.

R-E-S-P-E-C-T

This goes for you and the people you're reading. Honor your deck by treating it with care and taking tarot seriously. This is conveyed by where you keep your cards (in a dedicated container versus shoved in the bottom of your purse) and how you approach your readings (appreciating their potency versus mocking it). If the cards aren't taken seriously, they will respond in kind.

∞

My personal code of ethics and expectations around etiquette are woven throughout my work, from how I advertise my services and open every reading to the way questions are asked at the end. Whatever form your ethical code takes—as a page on your website or an entry in your journal—take the time to craft something that speaks to you. Think of it as a love letter to your deck; be clear with your intentions and outline what you hope to gain by working with the cards. Allow it to set the tone for how you show up in a reading... and in life.

CHAPTER 8

∞

Fools & Kings for Ding-a-Lings
(Arcana Architecture)

In a nutshell, a tarot deck has two major components: the Major Arcana and the Minor Arcana. Most decks today are styled after the *Rider-Waite-Smith*, *Thoth*, or *Marseille* systems. These cards may have different names and images distinguishing them, but they all contain a Major and Minor Arcana.

If you're thinking *WTF is an Arcana?* I've got you covered. And even if you're already familiar with the term, it's worth reexamining the Major and Minor Arcana—and common misconceptions that I find limiting.

The word "arcana" comes from the Latin *arcanus* (meaning "secret"), and it was used to describe mysteries of the spiritual and physical realms during the Middle Ages. Some believe that occultist Jean-Baptiste Pitois, writing under the pen name Paul Christian in the 1800s, applied Arcana to the cards in order to establish their mythical origins. The accuracy of this claim can't be verified, and

Pitois was known to fabricate historical facts to suit his theories, but what is certain is that by the time the *Rider-Waite-Smith* deck was published forty years later, tarot decks commonly contained both a Major and Minor Arcana.

ANATOMY OF THE ARCANA

Every tarot deck has seventy-eight cards: the Major Arcana, consisting of twenty-two numbered cards starting with The Fool at zero; and the Minor Arcana, which is composed of fifty-six cards divided into four suits, sometimes referred to as pips. The suits explore different dimensions of daily life (e.g., finances) and are generally a variation of Cups, Wands, Swords, and Pentacles (or Coins). Each suit contains cards numbered ace to ten, which symbolize beginnings that progress to completion, as well as four court cards that can represent influences and situations or actual people.

Traditionally, the Major Arcana is thought to convey more complex messages that express universal themes and experiences that carry more weight, while the Minor Arcana reflects those themes in different areas of daily life on a smaller scale (e.g., Death is transformational change, and the Five of Wands is the petty squabbling that can result from resisting change). To some extent I agree, but plenty of Minor cards deliver major messages, like the Five of Swords calling out our unattainable compulsion to be in control, or the opportunity for healing brought by the Six of Cups.

In general, the Major Arcana reflects aspects of your unconscious self while the Minor Arcana mirrors aspects of your life, but in my experience, you must consider these meanings in the context of where you are in life, how they're placed in the spread, and your interpretation. All play a huge role in the guidance you'll get from tarot. For me, the Ace of Swords is the most powerful card of the entire deck, while The Emperor is a total snooze. And a few of Major and Minor card pairings are kind of like siblings, with the Major card acting as the big brother or sister that blankets a situation, while its younger sibling (the Minor card) has a similar message—but as more of a towel than a blanket. Examples include Strength with the Nine of Wands and The Hermit with the Four of Swords (I'll elaborate in upcoming chapters). My point is this: Always remember that your individual interpretation is just as important as the standard definition, if not more.

BDE (THE MAJOR ARCANA)

The Major Arcana has all of the tarot headliners you're familiar with, including the ones that freak people out the most. The Devil, Death, and The Tower have been synonymous with kitschy soothsayer stereotypes for over a century: from the heroine's tragic demise being foretold in the opera *Carmen* in 1875 to a fortune-teller freaking out the ladies of Netflix's *Wine Country* in 2019.

The iconic images of the Major Arcana symbolize universal aspects of the collective experience. They represent archetypes that are consistent patterns of influence inherent to human nature. Our personal paths are unique, but certain milestones are universal. A Major Arcana card represents an energy that can be deep, strong, decisive, or long-term. In general, cards from the Major Arcana aren't messing around—they represent the big challenges, opportunities, and crossroads of life that can have a long-term impact. When the Major Arcana shows up, you'd better pay attention.

The Fool's Journey

As the protagonist of the Major Arcana, The Fool (card zero) invites you to join him on an expedition of self-discovery known as "The Fool's Journey." Every Major Arcana card he encounters on his mythical road to wholeness acts as a spiritual compass, leading him to life-altering wisdom that reveals different facets of our complex existence. Cosmic patterns are revealed throughout this introspective odyssey, helping him navigate the path to enlightenment.

The Fool's symbolic quest reflects the human experience, mirroring different stages of our personal development as we strive to understand why we're here, where we're going, and how to get there. The journey of The Fool may be structured within the Major Arcana, but our stories are not fixed, and the plot is ever-evolving.

NO SMALL PARTS (THE MINOR ARCANA)

While the thematic imagery of the Minor Arcana can vary—for example, bowling pins instead of wands—the framework remains consistent: four distinct suits that include court cards (traditionally Page, Knight, Queen, and King) and numbered cards starting at ace and going up to ten. The *Rider-Waite-Smith* deck was the first to introduce the descriptive imagery you'll find in the Minor Arcana of most modern decks.

The stories of the Minor Arcana typically deal with specific times of life or a particular opportunity for growth, as opposed to the cosmic connections found in the Major Arcana. But remember, just because the Minor cards aren't steeped in archetypes doesn't make them any less powerful. Below you'll see how each suit has its own vibe and tends to correspond with a distinct area of life (e.g., Pentacles and finance). That said, we'll dive into crossovers as we go card by card in upcoming chapters.

Wands

Most people love when a Wands card shows up, for good reason. Wands provide an energetic kick in the ass, inspiring and motivating us with their passionate enthusiasm. These sparkly sticks bring a bold and tenacious energy to every reading. They're often career-oriented and very creative, associated with intuition, ambition, and growth.

Wands represent beginnings, so it makes sense that spring is their season and newly sprouting buds on branches are common in their iconography. They're also associated with the element of fire and the corresponding astrological signs of Aries, Leo, and Sagittarius.

If Wands were a person, ideal careers would include life coach, serial entrepreneur, or professional cheerleader. The other suits help to stabilize and give form to this firecracker energy so it doesn't fizzle out after the first rush of inspiration.

Cups

Cups signify feelings in all forms, with joy and sorrow getting equal billing. The water in these Cups runs deep, symbolizing love, spirituality, and the subconscious. Cups connect us in relation to each other and our higher selves.

Their focus on empathy, the unconscious, and psychic spaces makes Cups align perfectly with Cancer, Scorpio, and Pisces. The fluidity of Cups makes water the obvious element, and summer is their season.

If Cups were a person, their best professions would be couples counselor, writer, or café barista. Since uncontained water can overflow and drown all in its path, the other signs offer some much-needed balance.

Swords

Swords aren't screwing around. These are generally serious cards and they mean business, with sharp edges that convey courage and conflict, logic and lessons, action and ideating. This suit is a powerful confluence of brains *and* brawn.

A lot of people break out in a sweat when Swords show up (Ten of Swords is no picnic), and these cards can definitely be challenging, but they're also necessary for our evolution and expansion. They may stress you out, but they also make you think.

Autumn is the season of Swords, air is their element, and the astrological affiliations are Gemini, Libra, and Aquarius. As a person, Swords would be a natural lawyer, inventor, or tech entrepreneur. Sword energy cuts through the bullshit to get to the truth, and the other suits can temper these blunt edges.

Pentacles (Coins)

Pentacles get shit done (and make bank while doing it). This industrious suit epitomizes hard work and has a practical, stable energy that usually corresponds with money and material matters. Whether in relation to career or another area of life, Pentacles' pragmatic vibe helps develop ideas and direct them into abundant reality.

The physical world is represented by Pentacles; it is the foundation for the creative, emotional, and intellectual pursuits of the other suits. Although tarot decks have included coins (or discs) since the beginning, the *Rider-Waite-Smith* deck first introduced Pentacles as a suit featuring the pentagram, or five-pointed star.

This sacred symbol has been around since ancient Egyptian times and was the personal brand of Greek philosopher Pythagoras. A pentagram demonstrates the golden ratio in mathematics and, during the Middle Ages, represented the five knightly virtues of friendship, generosity, chastity, courtesy, and piety. Pentagrams can be found in many cultures and religions, from Christianity to Islam, while modern Wiccans relate it to the intrinsic magic found throughout the natural world. It wasn't until the 1960s that pentagrams were repurposed as satanic symbols, giving Pentacles (and tarot) a bad rap.

The grounded, generous energy of Pentacles aligns beautifully with the element of earth, season of winter, and the astrological signs of Taurus, Virgo, and Capricorn. As a person, Pentacles would be a great financial adviser, heart surgeon, or luxury retail magnate.

NUMEROLOGY

Now that you have a sense of the Minor Arcana suits, it's time to look at their numbers and what they signify. In numerology, each digit between 1 and 9 has its own unique meaning, and when brought together, the sequences also have special significance. You can go down a numerology wormhole—but it's perfectly fine to focus on the story of each card without layering on extra meanings with numbers. That said, even a basic understanding of the universal meanings behind numbers can add depth to your readings.

Every suit has ten cards, starting with ace. Each number reveals a pattern with a similar structure that plays out in different ways, depending on the suit. If you see multiples of specific numbers in a reading, that's an invitation to look at how certain themes might be repeating in your life.

Ace

An ace is the strongest representation of a suit because it's number one and has yet to be divided. The ace of any suit expresses the intrinsic nature of that suit in its purest form. Aces signify beginnings that are full of promise; one is the number of power and potential from which everything else grows.

2

When the pure energy of an ace is split in half equally, you get two. The number two reveals conflict with opportunities for balance. It represents the power of opposites (calm versus chaos, pain versus pleasure, etc.) and the chance to create equilibrium.

3

Within three you may find initial efforts paying off with the completion of a first stage, but there is still work to be done. This is an expansive number, symbolizing the growth that is possible despite potential obstacles.

4

The solid sides of a square are represented by four. It's a very sturdy number with a rejuvenating energy that is grounded in healing and fortification, but care must be taken to not let stability morph into stagnation.

5

The balance of four is challenged by the uncertainty of five. This number introduces fluctuation, conflict, and adversity, but there is a motive behind this madness because out of the chaos comes an opportunity for growth. Pushing past instability leads to evolution. The setbacks are temporary, but the change is lasting.

6

After the storms of five, six brings the rainbow. This number is imbued with a sense of harmony and flow. Solutions are found through letting go, difficulties are overcome, and reconciliation is possible.

7

Seven offers the opportunity to take a stand and overcome challenges, gaining wisdom and confidence along the way. Objectives are met by tapping into the leader within. Independent effort is required, whether that means stepping back to assess or taking decisive action.

8

The experience gained with seven is put to the test by eight. This number reflects regeneration, progress, and commitment. Opposing forces are balanced as we push past internal and external limitations.

9

Nine is the highest single-digit number, symbolizing completion or endings. This sense of finality can be viewed as positive or negative, but either way it's necessary for the transformation that awaits with ten. Nine synthesizes everything learned in the numbers leading up to it, culminating in the full realization of a suit's energy.

10

Ten makes way for the launch of a new cycle, acting as the epilogue for each suit. It indicates the transformation that has occurred, whether attaining bliss (Cups and Coins) or overcoming hardship

(Swords and Wands). Ten offers a chance to celebrate the wins and reflect on the lessons before embarking on a new beginning.

∞

It might help to divide the Minor Arcana number sequence into four phases: Ace to three is the launch, four to six is optimization, seven to nine is fulfillment, and ten is transformation.

COURT CARDS

Court cards are notoriously tricky to decipher, particularly the Pages and Knights, because they could represent you, another person, certain occupations or situations, abstract energies, or just, like, vibes. There are a few visual cues—a sword here, a fish there—and certain identifiers, such as age or appearance. You can also look at the suit for clues, such as the passionate and charming qualities of Wands as compared to the emotional and dreamy Cups. But tarot newbies often get lost in the sauce trying to force a court card's personality traits onto people they know (never mind an event or set of circumstances).

I used to *hate* court cards. They were by far the most frustrating cards for me to work with, and I dreaded pulling them. That changed when I gave up on associating Pages and Knights with people and started connecting them to messages, influences, or lessons. I also determined that Kings and Queens were *always* people, usually expressing an aspect of the person being read. (Remember, Kings and Queens are never defined by gender but rather by personality attributes that are pulled to the surface in a reading.) Once I adapted these meanings within the essence of the suit, readings became much easier . . . and infinitely better. I've included the general explanations for each court category below, and we'll get into my interpretations in the suit-specific chapters.

Page

Sometimes referred to as Knave or Princess, the Page symbolizes discovery and new ideas. The energy is young, inexperienced, and eager to explore everything the suit has to offer—like an innocent tween who hasn't fully developed but is *very* curious. Pages are not quite ready to follow through with the action of their suit's specific energy (e.g., the Page of Cups needs to cultivate emotional vulnerability, while the Knight of Cups is writing poems and proposing marriage). Like the Knights, they have specific meanings instead of being stand-ins for real people.

Knight

A Knight (sometimes called Prince) is all action, ready to set the Page's ideas in motion. This fiery energy is impatient, impulsive, and often unpredictable. Although they never represent actual people in my readings, Knights have the intense energy of a hormonal teenager; they want to prove themselves and often act before thinking things through. It can be equal parts enthusiastic and exhausting.

Queen

When a Queen shows up, it's not indicating that her personality is you, but rather that her characteristics are being drawn out of you based on the question you're asking or in relation to the cards around her. The Queens represent the four female archetypes: the maiden (Cups), the mother (Wands), the queen (Swords), and the crone (Pentacles). Queen energy is traditionally more inward-facing compared to their King counterparts, who take external action. The Queens are mature rulers in their own right, with a deep understanding of the strengths and challenges of their suit.

King

Like the Queens, a King can represent a person generically or in the context of someone's character. Kings take action in measured and thoughtful ways (as opposed to the Knight's rash approach), and they've mastered the essence of their suit through practical application rather than introspection.

∞

As you go through the court card hierarchy from Page to King, it might help to consider how each stage—through the lens of their respective suits—experiences the world with increasing levels of awareness and understanding. From a suit perspective, Wands offer an initial spark of energy to a person or situation, while Cups nurture it with emotional support, and Swords logically organize the process, allowing Pentacles to usher it into the physical realm.

Through the Major and Minor Arcana, tarot cards connect us to the unknown—whether that's a universal intelligence, our inner wisdom, or the energy of the Divine. I give equal importance to both because the Minor can lead to the same kind of impactful insights, profound healing, and lasting shifts as the Major. What the Minor Arcana lacks in larger archetypal themes, it makes up for in specificity that is often just as powerful. Both instruct us in navigating the challenges and opportunities we encounter while also explaining why they might be showing up in the first place.

CHAPTER 9

∞

Towers & Devils & Death, Oh My!
(The Major Arcana)

Every card in the Major Arcana is a stepping stone on the path to wholeness, unlocking secrets to help you reveal your purpose and step into your potential. A universal human experience that is expressed through a story in the Major Arcana can be applied to a thousand different people and resonate with each in deeply personal ways. These stories can accompany life-changing transitions or precede pivotal moments, but their messages can also be more mundane.

The Major Arcana represent monumental, groundbreaking influences. These dynamic cards typically appear during major transitions, signaling distinctive moments of transformation. The cards are numbered, beginning with The Fool at zero, to reflect the passage of time.

What follows is a breakdown of these twenty-two cards, a starting point on your own tarot journey, including the conventional interpretations as well as my own personalized meaning. But what you deduce from these cards is just as crucial as what you're about to read. Take what works for you and leave what doesn't. Let your intuition guide you to initiate your own discourse with your deck.

For some cards, I might share a particular ritual to help you get the most out of the message. If you want to go deeper, you'll find a whole world of rituals to complement your tarot practice in my first book.

THE FOOL (0)

The Fool tells you to leap and
the net will appear.

The Fool isn't about being stupid or doing foolish things; it's urging you to take that first step without knowing how things will end up (or even what the second step looks like).

This card wants you to have faith in yourself and start with a single step, which often requires a bit of blissful ignorance and blind optimism.

You're being called to move from a place of inaction to action. Get momentum going so that the Universe has something to get behind. Don't carry the burden of planning, visualizing, and predetermining the next step—let the Universe play a role in the process (which, spoiler alert, is happening whether you realize it or not).

Remember that we don't know what we don't know, and the Universe has a better plan for us than we have for ourselves. Think back to a time in your life when you got what you wanted and thought, *Holy crap—I'm exactly where I want to be, but how it happened was unbelievable!* The Universe is on the sidelines saying, *Yeah, I know . . . I was there too, remember?*

Take these moments in your past as proof to help you have faith that they could happen again moving forward. I've spent my fair share of time daydreaming in front of a vision board, wondering why nothing was happening. It was only when I got off my butt and started moving in the direction of my dreams that things shifted. Procrastination is an alluring shield for our fears, doubts, and insecurities. It's so much easier and safer to focus on perfecting the plan, but "progress over perfection" is my motto.

I've seen in my own life and in the lives of countless clients how the smallest steps can kick-start the big picture. And more often than not, when we take those brave first steps (make the call, sign up for the class, write the résumé), we end up creating a reality beyond our wildest dreams.

The vibe of The Fool is like standing on a diving board and looking into the pool, thinking, *Is there water down there? Is it safe for me to jump? I can't see!* The Fool is telling you that of course you can jump because there *is* water in the pool—you just don't know the temperature. But it's not boiling water, nor is it ice . . . it's something you can handle.

You won't know until you jump.

THE MAGICIAN (I)

The Magician offers a master class in manifesting.

The Magician needs you to believe in your ability to create the life you want and then get off your ass and make it happen. He stands strong, holding his wand triumphantly in the air as he fiercely proclaims *I'm The Magician and I can do anything!* He has all of his tools—Wand, Cup, Sword, and Coin—on the table before him and he's ready to make magic. But if ten years down the road he's still standing there whining about his powers without picking up his tools, he's wasting his magical mojo.

This is a card of manifesting, but don't get it twisted: Intention is nothing without inspired action. The Universe isn't an indulgent fairy godmother granting every wish just because you journaled about it and walk around acting like you already have it.

There are a lot of self-proclaimed gurus out there promoting blind faith and fueling broken dreams, if only you believe hard enough. This leads to a bunch of ding-a-lings sitting in front of their vision boards wondering why the thing they want hasn't happened yet (confession: I used to be one of those ding-a-lings).

The Magician tweaks this approach. Yes, you must believe boldly in your intentions—you can daydream, journal, or make a vision board—but you also have to start moving in the direction of your dreams to kick-start momentum that the Universe can get behind. Then be open to recognizing the synchronicities and stepping stones that show up seemingly out of nowhere to guide you to your goal . . . or lead you to something better.

Dreams become reality with effort, but that doesn't necessarily mean toiling away for decades. When you're aligned with your purpose, the work you're doing may not seem that hard because it makes your heart and soul so happy. This is how you connect with your true purpose—start with a goal and work toward it while being open to whatever else might show up. Consider it an invitation for the Universe to put you in alignment with your potential, revealing what you *need* as opposed to what you so desperately *want*.

That's the secret sauce to this card: combining clear intention with inspired action, then getting out of your own way. Are you ready to make some magic?

THE HIGH PRIESTESS (II)

The High Priestess needs you to plug into your internal GPS.

Intuition can be challenging to work with because it often shows up as a soft whisper that's easy to miss (as opposed to the fearful judgement of our noisy egos). The High Priestess wants you to be more proactive, rather than reactive, with your intuition so you can start using it to your advantage. Rituals are a great way to do this.

My favorite method to access intuition is writing wild (also known as automatic writing). All you need is a notebook and pen, along with a timer set for five minutes, which seems like a long time, but I promise it will go quickly once you get going.

Start by quieting your mind with a brief meditation or even just a few deep breaths. Then pick up your pen and begin writing. Jot down whatever comes through without questioning or censoring yourself.

Even if the thoughts or words are totally unrelated, write them down. If you're drawing a blank, just write "I don't know what to write" over and over until something else shows up. If you're thinking, *This is dumb*—write that down. The key is to write without thinking until the timer signals that you're done. Forget about spelling and how it looks, and don't worry if it's politically incorrect or irrational. Just let it flow knowing that you can rip it up and throw it away later.

After the time is up, take a minute to read through what you've written and note anything that jumps out at you as a new insight. You might only receive a small nugget of relevant information, and that's okay—trust that more intel may come through in the coming days, especially if you commit to this practice consistently. Do it every morning before breakfast or last thing at night (or a different time every day), but try to do it daily because you may find yourself receiving guidance on Thursday for something you asked about on Monday. Or you may see answers and opportunities show up that relate directly to what you've written. I've experienced this countless times in my own life, to the point that it kind of freaks me out (which, to be clear, takes a lot in my line of work).

When The High Priestess appears in a reading, she's inviting you to tap into your higher wisdom. Step back, get quiet, and hear what that little voice has to say. Your intuition is speaking to you. Your only job is to listen.

THE EMPRESS (III)

The Empress is a literal and metaphorical baby-maker.

The Empress is a juicy card of fertility, often related to marriage, motherhood, and domestic life.

Although The Empress doesn't guarantee getting knocked up (remember, no predictions here), if this card shows up when you are trying for a baby by whatever means (pregnancy, surrogacy, or adoption), the energy around it is really encouraging.

If your reaction to parenthood is more like *Absolutely Not*, keep in mind that getting The Empress doesn't mean you're destined to be pregnant (but please take note, protection-wise, if applicable);

she can also symbolize other aspects of life at home, such as your family unit or buying a new house.

Alternatively, The Empress can also signal fresh starts, new paths, and exciting opportunities in other areas of life, such as your career or relationships.

My mom was sixty-three years old when she divorced my dad (better late than never . . .), and she thought she'd have to leave town because everyone in her social circle was either part of their married-couple friend group or a relative of my father.

She was retired (so, no work buddies), hadn't made a new friend in years, and had no hobbies or interests of her own because weekends had revolved around my dad's golf obsession. For the first time in her life, my mom had no one to answer to but herself.

That's how "Operation Grandma Gets Her Groove Back" began. It was a journey of self-discovery that my sister and I privately referred to as "Spring Break for Seniors" because she was determined to make up for lost time (and she had a lot of ground to cover).

My formerly sedentary mother was now rock climbing, buying a pool cue for her billiards league, and attending "Live Music for Boomers" every weekend. She often couldn't talk when I called because "I'm at a Ping-Pong tournament and it's my serve."

My kids don't recognize pictures of my mom holding them as babies because she's since lost forty pounds, colored her hair, and looks twenty years younger. To my tarot clients who find themselves faced with a fresh start, I often tell my mom's story of new beginnings because her journey reassures them that anything is possible, and if she can do it, anyone can.

When The Empress shows up in a reading, you need to harness her creation energy and channel it in the direction of your dreams. Whether making a baby in your body, launching a new initiative, or heading down a new path, The Empress is here to tell you those seeds are being planted in *very* fertile soil.

THE EMPEROR (IV)

The Emperor is as dry as The Empress
is juicy.

The Emperor is the masculine counterpart to The Empress. He exudes stability, control, and security—not necessarily a bad thing, but definitely not as sparkly as some other cards.

Traditionally, this card calls for more structure in your life. In my readings, The Emperor usually represents a place of business, organization, or institution. It's where you work, the bank, the military, or the government. He can be a school, hospital, or court of law. Basically, if there's a building involved, it's The Emperor in action (or rather, inaction).

Every so often The Emperor shows up as masculine energy in

human form, like the Kings of the Minor Arcana. If he *is* representing a person, he has the sturdy and staid energy of a building or institution—conventional, traditional, and stuck in his ways. He doesn't have to be an old man, but he definitely has old man energy. He can be a man or The Man. When this curmudgeonly card shows up, I usually pull another one for context, just like I would for a King or Queen, because he's not telling me much on his own.

Although he can be a bit dull, The Emperor does serve a purpose in our lives. He sets boundaries, cultivates discipline, and works hard to get things done. Again, these aren't necessarily detriments, and might be what you need to hear in the moment, they're just not super sexy.

THE HIEROPHANT (V)

The Hierophant is a boring card that
can be about exciting things.

Also known as the Pope, The Hierophant is a counterpart of The High Priestess, and it's a raging case of opposites attract. Where The High Priestess is all dreams and intuition, The Hierophant is tradition and convention to the core.

The Hierophant historically has a religious element, but in my readings, he's all business all the time. I envision this card as a never-ending inbox, piled high with documents that require your attention—paperwork, applications, legal documents, and other drudgery. It's the kind of writing that would give you carpal tunnel if it weren't digitized.

The Hierophant can represent the schoolwork of a teacher or student, signing contracts (for a new house!) or settlements (for an old husband!). He can symbolize writing presentations for a new client or creating a business plan for your next chapter. The work might not be exciting, but the outcome could be the manifestation of your dreams.

Like his buddy The Emperor, The Hierophant isn't the most thrilling card in the deck, but he gets the job done. Or, more likely, he's imploring *you* to get it done.

THE LOVERS (VI)

The Lovers card is all about
sexy times.

The Lovers signals more than good friends—it's friends with benefits. Although traditional tarot decks depict a man and woman, The Lovers represents romantic love between any two (or more!) people of any persuasion in any situation.

This can be a romantic relationship in the past, present, or future—depending on the question asked, the cards around it, or where it appears in a spread. The Lovers can represent Mr. Right or Mr. Right-for-Tonight, the love of your life or a flirtation in the making. It can be a full-fledged affair, a long-term relationship, or lusting from afar, but make no mistake: People are getting naked (if only in their fantasies).

THE CHARIOT (VII)

The Chariot brings you
big choices.

Two beasts are held, one in each hand and each going in a different direction, and if a decision isn't made, the driver will be ripped in two. The Chariot traditionally signifies success, willpower, and determination (think Russell Crowe in the original *Gladiator* movie, entering the Colosseum to the cheers of an adoring crowd).

For me, this card represents big decisions to be made on the path to success. The key to making the right choice is to avoid thinking everything to death while also not letting emotions rule you. Let your gut have a say because that's where your intuition lives.

This doesn't mean relying solely on instinct; let your intuition, intellect, and emotion all have seats at the decision-making table. A quick exercise to access all three is to sit where nobody will disturb you, ground yourself with some deep breaths, and close your eyes as you imagine taking each path. Activate as many of your senses as possible as you visualize yourself in every option, then notice how you feel. Is there a pinch in your neck or are there butterflies in your belly? Are you smiling or trying not to barf? Notice how your body reacts because it will give you clues—and one option will always feel better (or less gross) than the other.

When you get still and let your imagination take over, the right choice will make itself known. You simply have to pay attention, be open, and trust.

STRENGTH (VIII)

Strength reminds you that you're
stronger than you think.

This is the strongest card in the deck, and it tends to show up when we need it most. It can indicate the strength of a bond or opportunity (depending on the cards around it and the question being asked), but it usually pertains to the person being read. If your strength—physical, spiritual, or emotional—has been tested recently, trust that you have it in spades. Don't sweat it and never forget it.

The infinity symbol signifies that you have a limitless well of strength to draw upon. Within you is a bedrock of strength supporting you through tough times. Where other people say it's too hard and they want to give up, you're ready to keep going.

Many people get emotional when this card comes up because they're at a low point, feeling tired and helpless. When you have a visceral reaction to a card (like tears or sighing), it's a reflection of how much the card and its meaning resonate with you in the moment. There's that mirror again, showing you a part of yourself from a new vantage point. Have a cry if you need to, then get back up and keep going.

You have strength for days—you just needed a reminder.

THE HERMIT (IX)

The Hermit needs you to embrace your inner Zen to get the guidance you need.

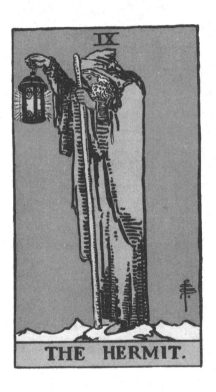

You're being asked (or shouted at, if you also pull the Four of Swords) to put down the electronics, step away from the busyness, disengage from the to-do list, and go within.

The answers you're looking for are inside you, but you can't access them when you're stuck in that superficial layer of life (*I have to feed-the-kids-walk-the-dog-buy-the-thing* . . .). You've been treading water and The Hermit wants you to take a deep dive.

Think about a time you were driving and arrived at your destination with no clue how you got there because your mind was off solving the world's problems. That's the kind of zone The Hermit wants you to explore (just not while driving because that's dangerous). You don't have to sit and meditate for hours—it can be as simple as going for a walk, doing yoga, or simply sitting with your eyes closed for a few minutes listening to yourself breathe.

It's often the rather mundane tasks—like driving, folding laundry, gardening—that allow you to zone out. While your brain and body are occupied, your subconscious can get to work. Whether it's meditation, knitting, vacuuming, or fishing—whatever encourages your mind to wander—The Hermit wants you doing more of that. The guidance you're looking for is waiting to be discovered.

WHEEL OF FORTUNE (X)

The Wheel of Fortune helps you make your own luck.

Traditionally, this card symbolizes a turn in luck and shifting tides. For me, it's the luckiest card in the deck. (The Sun, The Star, and The World also bring lucky vibes to a reading.) The Wheel of Fortune is like a wave of good mojo coming up behind you, and you need to hop on and ride it like a surfer rather than letting it wash over you. My luck cards don't just hand you good fortune—there are lessons to be learned that help you harness the lucky vibes and make the most of them.

The Wheel of Fortune teaches us that we're born at A and we

die at Z. Many people move through life in a straight line, heads down and blinders on, like passive passengers on a bus. But the Wheel of Fortune invites you to open yourself to what's possible, offering the chance for a much more dynamic and meaningful journey.

If you've embraced the lessons of The Magician—setting clear intentions, taking inspired action, and stepping aside to let life flow—your path can transform into something unexpected and extraordinary.

When you're co-creating with the Universe, your journey is no longer a straight line from A to Z. Instead, it's full of fascinating loops and exciting squiggles. You've moved from being a passenger to becoming the driver of your own bus.

The Wheel of Fortune reminds you that you're on the bus, and manifesting is how you transition from passenger to driver—that's how you leverage the luck before you.

When I was a twenty-year-old university student, I bought a ticket to Australia with no clue how I'd pay for the actual trip. Fresh off a breakup, I decided to skip the usual post-split rituals (getting ill-advised bangs or partying with my girlfriends) and instead dropped a semester's tuition to travel across the planet.

With only four months until departure and a part-time cashier job, I needed to make money—fast. I found full-time work as a receptionist and spent every spare moment researching hostels, but I still came up short.

My only option was selling my car—a fifteen-year-old Datsun hatchback my friends lovingly called the Turdmobile. I would've been lucky to get a few hundred dollars for it, and the cost of a classified ad (this was way before computers) ate into any potential profits. Desperation was setting in.

Three people came to see the car, but none made an offer.

One guy even slowed down to take a look, then just kept driving. Despite the setbacks, I stayed focused on the bigger picture—planning my itinerary, packing my gear, and trusting that things would somehow work out.

Ten days before my departure, I got extremely lucky: My car was stolen. A few days later, the police recovered it, completely trashed and undrivable (basically how it was before, but the cops didn't need to know that). I tried to hide the relief in my voice when the insurance adjuster told me the damages were so extensive the car was a write-off.

The payout? Three thousand dollars.

Even today, three grand would stretch pretty far on a backpacker's budget. In 1990, it funded nearly a year of travel. It was a master class in manifesting—and the Wheel of Fortune in action—long before I even knew what those things meant.

JUSTICE (XI)

*Justice serves karmic cause
and effect.*

Even when there are legal matters at hand, Justice reminds you that karma ebbs and flows like the tide—what you put out is what you get back.

If you put out your best effort, it will come back to you. Maybe not as quickly as you'd like (because we all want it yesterday), and it won't look how you expected it to (because it never does), but it will return to you. When you're half-assing things or phoning it in, the results will reflect your efforts. For example, if I decide to get in the best shape of my life and join a gym, but then sit on the couch doing nothing for six months, I'll see the consequences of my actions (less money in my pocket and no progress in my fitness).

Justice is also here to remind you that karma is like farming—it's not sexy, and there are no shortcuts or gimmicks. You need to get up, show up, do the work, and wait for your harvest to come in. Karmic Justice applies to all areas of life—love, wealth, health, family, etc. The message isn't exciting, but it is universal: Output and effort yield results. And don't get sidetracked worrying about anyone else's karma because that's being sorted out and it's none of your business.

This card is one of two in the deck that has a cranky grandpa vibe, as if to say *Put your boots on, stop messing around, and get to work!* (The Four of Cups is the other one.) Listen to the old grump—you'll thank yourself later.

THE HANGED MAN (XII)

The Hanged Man wants you to
go with the flow.

Although it looks disturbing on the surface, The Hanged Man is only killing time. He's swinging back and forth like a pendulum, hanging by his foot (not his head). This card urges patience on your part.

That light around his head indicates that if you can *let* life happen instead of trying to *make* it happen, you'll be rewarded. This doesn't mean sitting like a lump doing nothing; it's a reminder to approach life with more grace and ease. You can't force timelines or determine outcomes, so release the need to be in control because that's anxiety.

When you try to bend time to fit arbitrary schedules, it's like trying to swim upstream: You get tired and cranky until you end up floating the way you were supposed to go from the start. Avoid that nonsense. Go with the flow.

Nothing teaches patience like being a parent (although having a puppy comes close). When my son was born, I learned that milestones like walking and talking were expected by certain ages. Other moms loved sharing how they had the walkiest, talkiest kids ever, and these critical deadlines that my son wasn't meeting stressed me out.

Despite assurances from my doctor that everything was on track development-wise, I was consumed with my kid's lack of progress—until a beautiful, foul-mouthed grandma at the park saved me from myself. I mentioned my concern over a skill my son was supposed to have mastered that month, and she let me know in no uncertain terms that I sounded like a crazy person.

"Don't be so fucking worried if your kid is keeping up," she said. "By the time he's in college he'll be able to make himself a sandwich, tie his shoes, and wipe his own ass—he'll be fine."

These words changed my entire approach to parenting—I'd been looking at it as a sprint instead of a marathon. I started to meet my son where he was at at any given moment, and twenty years later, he graduated college able to make a sandwich, tie his shoes, and wipe his own ass with confidence.

DEATH (XIII)

Death is the most misunderstood card of the deck.

Death is not the scary, IBS-inducing card you think it is. It's one of my favorite cards to get in a reading. Before I lay out a single card, I always reassure people that the Death card never predicts physical death of any kind—no animals, plants, or people. Just like every other card in the deck, this one offers context around your situation and how to navigate the energies around you.

I've heard of tarot readers who delight in telling people about the impending passing of loved ones, and it's also a common pop-culture cliché, but it's unnecessary and lazy and, in all likelihood, untrue.

Spoiler alert: We're all going to die. Trying to predict death is like guessing lottery numbers—you're wrong more often than you're right. And it scares the crap out of people along the way. I'm more interested in helping you make this one life the best one possible instead of forecasting when it's going to end. (Even if someone *could* give you that kind of information, what are you supposed to do with it?)

The Death card is about transformational change coming your way. The Sun in the distance validates change that is positive and necessary. What makes this card so scary is your relationship with change. If you embrace change with an *I'm ready, let's do this!* attitude, it can be fantastic from start to finish. If you resist change and don't adapt easily, it might suck the entire way. The result is still positive, but the process to get there is harder than necessary.

This card asks you to embrace change despite the inherent discomfort that usually comes with any kind of change. It's like a Band-Aid coming off—are you going to pull it in one quick motion that you barely notice, or will you pull it off slowly, feeling every hair?

How you experience this card is very much up to you.

TEMPERANCE (XIV)

Temperance is evidence of
your angels at work.

Temperance used to be the most boring card in the deck for me, and now it's the one I talk about the most during a reading. It's a prime example of how the dialogue with your cards evolves over time to offer a deeper, more insightful tarot experience.

Typically, this card asks for balance. Whether that balance is between thinking and feeling, work and play, or something else, Temperance wants you to take it easy because equilibrium is the goal.

In my readings, we go in a very different (and more profound) direction. Temperance reminds you that the energy of angels, guides, and those who have passed is surrounding you, like indulgent parents ready to shower you with love and support. Your team of light is encouraging you to engage with them, and pulling this card is your opportunity to do just that. (It might also be the sign you've been asking for.)

People often have their own ways of connecting with this angelic energy, but I always share the approach I've developed over time. I refer to it as the Three *A's* of Angels: ask, acknowledge, and allow.

First you have to *ask*, whether that's dancing naked under a Full Moon, talking to Grandma while brushing your teeth, praying on your knees at an altar, or finding another way that resonates. You can ask for guidance, healing, reassurance, or something else, but don't get tied to timelines or attached to specific outcomes. Ask for help finding your ideal partner or for support in your upcoming job interview—and if it takes more time than you'd prefer to find that person or you don't get that job, it doesn't mean your angels weren't listening. Have faith that your team of light is working to get you the best possible outcome.

When you put out the call, you'll always get a response, but instead of talking or touching, angel energy communicates in signs that you must *acknowledge* in order to keep the channel of communication open. Signs are everywhere; you simply have to ask and then be open to receiving them, which can happen in a variety of ways. Your sign might be goose bumps or feathers, chimes or dimes—whatever form your angelic signal takes, be open to noticing it.

The last and most important step (that we often screw up) is to *allow*. Once our prayers are answered and dreams start coming true, we tend to hit the energetic brakes by questioning how and why it's all happening. The momentum that was building grinds to a halt, and we're left with half-realized wishes. When this happens, you just have to breathe through it and remind yourself that you're worthy of these blessings. Your success doesn't deny anyone else's because there's enough for everybody. Also, and this is crucial, be sure to thank your angels and guides so you can move to the next item on your list (you've made a list by now, right?).

Temperance is the calling card of your angels. They're inviting you to ask, acknowledge, and allow.

THE DEVIL (XV)

The Devil isn't evil; he's just an asshole.

People freak out when they see this card and I always tell them there's nothing satanic or scary about it. Traditionally, The Devil conveys addictions, greed, lust, and other so-called deadly sins. For me, it goes deeper and addresses the underlying damage that is often externalized in destructive tendencies.

The Devil is your shadow side—the dream killer and energy drainer that lurks in the deepest recesses of your psyche, ready to pounce when your guard is down. Many people attempt to repress the shadow with everything from booze and drugs to shopping and sex. But these panaceas simply diminish your defenses as they deaden your feelings, feeding the shadow until it inevitably undermines and sabotages every area of your life.

When The Devil shows up in a reading, it's highlighting the part of you that feels unworthy of abundance. It's the voice in your head saying that things will never change because you don't deserve any better. It's the imposter syndrome confirming you don't belong, the self-sabotage that reaffirms your inadequacy, and the inner perfectionist that stops you from ever starting. Whether it's a persistent whisper or bellowing shriek, you need to understand that this voice isn't real. It just feels that way because you accepted it as true when you were very young, before you had the ability to discern it as utter bullshit.

It's only when you step into the darkness that you can discover your light. When you meet your shadow and bring it to the surface, profound shifts can occur. By identifying (rather than denying) those disturbing parts of yourself, you can experience real transformation on a soul level because you finally understand that the shame that was imposed on you was in fact a reflection of someone else's trauma and insecurities.

The Devil highlights the limiting beliefs and negative self-talk that prevent you from stepping into your power and living your best life.

You can stop The Devil in its tracks (or at least lower the volume) with some ritual homework that I've been assigning people for over thirty years:

> Sit in a quiet space and ground yourself with a few deep breaths as you visualize your devil. How does that voice in your head look, sound, and even smell? Once you have a clear sense of your devil in your mind, it's time to slaughter it:

Throw it off a bridge, flush it down the toilet, or just have it disintegrate in a puff of smoke. Feel free to get creative as you eliminate that shame-inducing voice that you've accepted your entire life without questioning if it's true.

Take a moment to notice how it feels to murder your inner mean girl. Is there a sense of lightness and liberation? Exhaustion or despair? Consider journaling about your experience to see what insights arise, and moving forward, be mindful when that voice comes back (because it's very difficult to extinguish completely). When you find yourself caught in a shame spiral or drowning in doubt, ask if what you're thinking is true or if it's your devil shit-talking in your ear. If it *is* your inner demon (spoiler: It usually is), then it's time for another metaphysical murder. This ritual is incredibly effective and easy to do once you realize how necessary it is.

By shining the light of awareness on your devil, you're cutting its power in half. Turning on the lights will reveal that the scary monster under your bed was just a harmless stuffed animal this whole time.

THE TOWER (XVI)

The Tower is life giving you
a wakeup call.

When The Tower shows up, it's highlighting the blinders you've been wearing regarding a person, situation, or the way you've been living your life—and it's time for them to come off. These blinders could relate to love, career, health, money, or any other area.

Going through life with blinders on isn't an authentic way to live, and The Tower removes them. The lightning that strikes The Tower is a flash of understanding—a realization that removes the veil so you can see things clearly. Unfortunately, the process of taking those blinders off can be painful, symbolized by the people getting thrown over the side, leaving you to wonder if you kicked puppies in a past life to warrant such suffering in this one. Thankfully, even if your Tower is an owie, it's usually a case of short-term pain for long-term gain.

At some point down the road, you'll gain the perspective to look back and think either *That was actually a blessing* or *That sucked, and I hated every second of it, but I get it*. Welcome to The Tower.

It can be a tragic and painful event (divorce, diagnosis, job loss) or something exciting and beautiful (winning the lottery, moving abroad, having a baby), but make no mistake: The Tower delivers breakdowns that often lead to breakthroughs. Regardless of how negative your struggles seem in the moment, they're shaping you for your purpose by teaching you lessons that must be learned.

The Tower shakes you to your core and is known by many names, including dark night of the soul, existential ennui, midlife crisis, or Saturn Return. Whatever you call it, and whether you perceive it as positive or negative, the disruptive energy of The Tower leads to growth that's never easy and sometimes painful—but is always necessary.

THE STAR (XVII)

The Star is your destiny.

The Star is traditionally a hopeful card that asks for self-reflection and renewal. In my readings, this is one of the four luckiest cards (along with the Wheel of Fortune, The Sun, and The World). To best benefit from this fortuitous energy, you need to learn the card's lesson. With The Star, it's understanding the role that destiny plays in your life.

People, opportunities, and experiences show up in your life because they're part of your path—that's your fate. What you choose to do in such a moment is often up to you because you have free will. You can dance with it or ignore it, learn from it, or let it kick your ass. Whether it lasts for twenty minutes or twenty years, it's happening for a reason and a season.

Don't spend too much time trying to figure out the deeper meaning behind why it's showing up; instead, grab some of that lucky stardust and stick it in your pocket so you can hit the road and do your thing. At some point along the way, you'll have more perspective about why things happened the way they did. Though we always want to know in advance rather than in retrospect, that's not how it works.

When it comes to destiny, consider this: We're born alone and we die alone, but from the start of our journey until the moment we pass, our souls join hands with other souls, such as family, friends, coworkers, and teachers. Sometimes, our souls walk hand in hand from start to finish. Other times, we split off only to reconnect years later. More often than not, our paths drift in different directions and we say "Our work here is done—see you on the other side."

The Star reminds you that we're all on individual paths. You can't drag people along their path or yank them onto yours, even when it's obvious you know better, because that messes with their karma. Trying to carry burdens that are not yours to bear can prolong or enlarge the lessons that others need to learn. You can only extend a hand and say "I'm here if you want to walk together on our respective paths, but I can't pull you along your path or force you onto mine . . . and I can't wait."

Understanding the role of destiny and free will, and not trying to live other people's lives for them, is how you capture the lucky energy of The Star.

THE MOON (XVIII)

The Moon needs you to set some energetic boundaries.

The energy of this card is like a can of baked beans being dumped into a pot a big sploosh of lumpy gunk. Conventional interpretations often focus on delusions, fears, and the unconscious. For me, The Moon highlights the energetic imbalance around you.

Every interaction with another person involves an energetic exchange, and invisible attachments are formed that will ideally dissolve once you part ways. Unfortunately, these etheric cords can sometimes remain long after we say goodbye. Think of the emotional vampire who leaves you needing a nap or a good cry. Or the energy dumpers who unload their crap on you, turning you into a rage monster. It's not usually malicious or intentional, but The Moon calls on you to be aware of these toxic attachments so you can deal with them before they start dealing with you, leaving you so depleted or overwhelmed that it manifests physically.

You can protect your energy in a variety of ways—have an end-of-day shower or visualize a protective light surrounding you—but cutting cords is the quickest means of energetic hygiene. The following exercise can be one of the most powerful practices in your spiritual toolbox:

> Find a quiet spot to close your eyes, and ground yourself in breath. Imagine shimmering, golden threads emanating from your heart center and floating to connect you with the heart of someone in your life who is an energy dumper or drainer. If you encounter a lot of people at your job, you can imagine multiple cords floating out into the ether, not necessarily connecting to a specific person. Gather them all up, grab an axe, sword, machete, or knife, and chop right through them. Visualize them snapping back like vacuum-cleaner cords. You aren't hurting anyone by doing this—you're simply restoring everyone's energy to a place of balance. You can even do it while visualizing your spouse or kids (they can be the most blatant offenders). Breathe deeply as you sever each cord, knowing that you are performing an act of service for everyone involved.
>
> Consider a restorative bath or shower to close your cord-cutting ritual and remember to drink plenty of water to cleanse your body from the inside out. Honoring your boundaries is an homage to the message of The Moon.

THE SUN (XIX)

The Sun is a hug from the Universe.

The Sun reassures you that you're doing an amazing job. This is a card of pure happiness, joy, and light—nourishing, loving, and protecting all of the cards around it. The Sun is also the best health card in the deck for me—not just physical health, but spiritual and emotional healing as well.

As one of the luckiest cards—in addition to the Wheel of Fortune, The Star, and The World—The Sun teaches a lesson to get at that luck and, although it sounds relatively simple, for me it was the hardest lesson of all.

To fully immerse yourself and marinate in The Sun's loving,

enthusiastic, lucky energy, you have to let that sunshine in. You need to allow, receive, and accept rather than deflect, reject, or minimize. When someone says you look amazing, don't respond with "Omigod I haven't slept in a month." Instead, say "Thank you." What you're really saying is "I welcome that. I honor and deserve it. More please. Keep it coming."

You must show the Universe that you are ready to receive and know how to allow—whether it's a compliment, a bank loan, a job, or a person. That's the key to harnessing the beautifully radiant, lucky energy of abundance that The Sun has to offer.

JUDGEMENT (XX)

Judgement is calling you on
your shit-talking.

This is traditionally a card of resurrection, spiritual growth, and renewal. In my readings, Judgement has a deeper story to tell because we must quiet the dragon within before we can ascend.

When Judgement appears in a reading, it's a clear call to silence your inner critic—there's way too much smack talk happening. Judgement reminds us that no matter how much we may criticize other people, we're always much harsher on ourselves. We'd never talk to our friends the way we often talk to ourselves because they'd be devastated (and also, we probably wouldn't think of them that way in the first place).

Perfectionism is a defense mechanism against shame. We're not here to be perfect; we're here to be whole—it can be a stinky, snotty, sweaty mess, but that's okay because we're doing the best we can with what we've got (and sometimes it's a gong show).

Consider how often you think or say "should"—it's such a shameful, demeaning word, and we're constantly should-ing all over ourselves. Replace your "should" with "could," "wish," or "want." *I should be more like this* becomes *I want to be like this*. Or *He should have done that* turns into *He could have done that*.

When you use the same harsh tone for the pairs of sentences above, the "shoulds" have way more sting; practice eliminating "should" from your vocabulary. Instead of *We should get sushi*, try *We could have sushi* or *I want sushi*—there are hundreds of ways to suggest sushi. This simple act of awareness can lead to the love and acceptance we all crave . . . with others and ourselves.

We're all a work in progress. Show yourself the compassion, forgiveness, patience, love, and kindness that you would extend to a child, sibling, or best friend. These small steps can start you on the path from shameful judgement to loving acceptance.

THE WORLD (XXI)

The World invites you to fail.

The World symbolizes success and the completion of goals. It's summiting the mountaintop and planting your flag triumphantly. But in my readings, one final lesson must be learned to secure any lingering luck: understanding the necessity of failure on the path to success.

Before success, there is opportunity. You've got the whole world in your hands. What will you do with it? Take a big, juicy bite? Or put it aside—because you're too busy, scared, or bored—only to realize years later that you missed the best part?

The World is here to remind you that this is your one life in this body in this moment, so go for it. Don't let fears of failing hold you back because failure is a requirement for success. People fail their way to success every single day, so focus instead on practice over perfection; otherwise, you risk stopping yourself before you even start.

When I took my kids ice-skating when they were young, I would always tell them that if they weren't on their butts for half the lesson, they wouldn't get a hot chocolate—because if they weren't falling, it meant they weren't trying.

You have to fall, fail, and crash because that's how you learn, grow, and adapt. Failure is the secret sauce of success. Don't just tolerate the idea of falling on your ass—embrace it, because falling means you're one step closer.

This isn't a dress rehearsal; it's your one life in this body at this moment. See your stumbles as learning opportunities and you'll harness the luck of The World to fuel your progress. It's like those old barn-wood signs you might see, proclaiming: *If You're Waiting for a Sign, This Is It.*

The World is your sign. You're ready. Get going. Make mistakes. Let failure be your fuel.

Dare to succeed.

∞

The Major Arcana tells the story of our collective and personal evolution. Each card symbolizes a pivotal stage on The Fool's path to enlightenment or self-actualization. Along the way, challenges are faced and lessons are learned, and in these stories, we see the reflection of our own fears and foibles as well as the potential for life-changing transformation.

Some of these archetypes will make a stronger impression on you than others, and your perception of them will likely shift over time. Be open to exploring how these cosmic connections resonate in your readings. And remember, they're meant to guide—not dictate—your journey.

As we explore the four suits of the Minor Arcana, we can build upon this wisdom to see how these so-called small-scale messages can still deliver powerful insight that resonates in deeply personal ways.

CHAPTER 10

∞

Hot Rods (Wands)

Wands have a primal energy, representing passion, purpose, and potential. They're generally accepted as the first suit of the Minor Arcana because they signify ideas and beginnings. Often related to career, Wands exude a vibrant, inspired, and charismatic vibe. They guide us to the driving forces of our personalities, highlighting what is best for us at the core of our being. Wands are associated with the season of spring and the element of fire as well as the astrological signs of Aries, Leo, and Sagittarius.

ACE OF WANDS

The Ace of Wands is passion personified.

The Ace of Wands is juicy, inspired energy in its purest form. It embodies fresh starts and new beginnings, fueled by a burst of motivation as you set off in a new direction or launch a project in any area of life. The imagery of this card often features flowers budding on the wand, which gives you a visual clue related to new beginnings.

The Ace of Wands is your purpose and potential. It opens the Big Book of You to a new chapter and an empty page to ask: *What are you going to write?*

Consider what makes your soul sing. What lights you up from the inside out? If you won the lottery and never had to work another day in your life, how would you spend your time (after getting the spa or travel out of your system)? You can't just sit and count your money all day, every day. Would you be writing? Taking care of animals? Playing pickleball?

When I was a little girl, I would line up my stuffed animals and use my little chalkboard to be their teacher (I created lesson plans and worksheets . . . it was a whole thing). I desperately wanted to be a teacher when I grew up.

When I wasn't giving math tests to my stuffies, I was putting on concerts for them. My room became my stage, with windows darkened and a little desk lamp shining on me. I performed my dad's Beach Boys live record as the tambourine-playing Beach Girl.

Four decades later, here I am: a professional tarot card reader.

What the heck does my current job have to do with my childhood obsessions of education and entertainment? Quite a lot, actually.

Every card in the deck provides a framework for me to teach my clients life lessons. I also lead tarot workshops, give readings at massive events, and speak about intuition and rituals on stages of all sizes. And let's not forget the performative aspect of reading tarot. While I may not dress like a fortune-teller from central casting, I definitely put on a bit of a show because I want people to have a good time while gaining the insight they need. In the quirkiest, most unexpected way, I've ended up with a job that echoes the things I loved as a little girl.

Clarity about your purpose can often be found in your past. Try exploring what lit you up as a little kid. When you were around eight years old and the adults told you to go play (and television wasn't an option), what did you gravitate toward? Would you pick up a book and get lost in the story? Pretend to be a soldier? Collect bugs? Draw?

Often we already have clues that can lead us to our purpose. Start recognizing what's in front of you, and trust that it's for you. Get curious about what makes time fly when you're doing it. The thing that you would do even if you weren't getting paid. Find that thread and pull on it to see where it takes you.

And remember, what pays your bills and what sparks joy in your heart and soul can be different things! Everyone says "Do what you love and the money will come," which is nice in theory, but you also need to make a living. If your day job facilitates the passion project that makes your heart happy, the day job becomes a lot more palatable.

Finding pleasure in your passions is the key to discovering your purpose. It's time to find your calling so you can answer the call. Listen to the story your soul is yearning to tell.

TWO OF WANDS

The Two of Wands needs you to get clear on your intentions.

This card is all about potential unfulfilled and continues the theme of new directions that connect to your life purpose and soul path. This explorer is holding a globe and looking out on the valley before him, trying to plan his next move. A world of possibility awaits, but he's still figuring out where he wants to go.

The Two of Wands lets you know that you're at the tip of the iceberg of your potential. There's so much for you to discover, but you have to get clear on your goal before you go. Otherwise, it's like setting out on a road trip without a map and no sense of direction—you could end up circling the block for years.

Where your focus goes, the energy flows, and you must kick-start momentum by determining your objective (this could be in one or many areas of life). If you're still struggling to find your target ten years later, you'll end up like the tube dude balloon guy that sits outside the hot tub store flopping around without getting anywhere.

This is the *What do I want to be when I grow up* card, and it applies regardless of your age because it's not about how you make your money—it's about how you live your life. Who you become is an ever-evolving process.

Any action you take is preceded by intention. Since your intention impacts the outcome, you need to get clear on what you want. Get the ball rolling on the path to your potential by choosing a goal. Start with a decision to do something or learn something or be something without worrying about how it will all go down.

When you know what you want and why you want it, the how will reveal itself.

THREE OF WANDS

The Three of Wands wants you to plan the work so you can work the plan.

This card's imagery features the same figure as the Two of Wands, but he's changed his outfit, ditched the globe, and has a wand in hand, ready to start his journey. He's still looking over that valley, but he now has a clear destination in sight: By setting an intention, he's one step closer to realizing his objective.

The next part is simple, but it can take years: Get off your butt and *go*. You don't have to jump across that valley on the first step; just get your toe on the path. Focus on a single step and don't worry if it's the first of five hundred steps. Don't try to take them all at once because even if that one step doesn't go where you expected, or you seem to go backwards, another step will reveal itself eventually.

You can hop on a new path once you get going, but first you need to go so you aren't standing there ten years later thinking, *Yep, that's where I'm headed. That's what I'll do. As soon as this is done and that's ready and that's perfect . . . then I'll do it.* The Three of Cards is saying "It's time to start moving in the direction of your dreams." Baby steps count. Go.

FOUR OF WANDS

The Four of Wands says, "If you don't want to burn out, stop living like you're on fire."

The conventional meaning of this card is celebrating success achieved after hard work—often signified in the form of a vacation—but for me, it drills deeper. Success can be hard to come by when you're running on empty. And it may be short-lived if you're falling apart. You might not even be able to appreciate success because you're burnt out. In order to attain and celebrate your goals, you need to be well-resourced from within.

In my readings, the Four of Wands focuses on self-care, and I don't mean pedicures and facials (but also: Get the facial). The Four of Wands needs you paying more attention to your energetic time management.

Your energy—physical, emotional, and spiritual—is like a balloon. If you're constantly giving this energy to friends, family, work, etc., all that will be left is a flat, empty balloon—and that can manifest physically, making you sick.

You need to fill your balloon, and it doesn't have to be a month in Bali: Go for a walk, read a book for pleasure, sleep in for twenty minutes. Understand that the time you allocate to yourself is more important than the time you spend on everyone and everything else. You might have to block it in your schedule, but you need to start from a full tank in order to be the best parent, partner, friend, boss, employee, and all of the other roles we assume. Repositioning yourself from last to first can be very difficult; reframing it as the way to make ourselves better for everyone and everything else can help alleviate the guilt we often feel (especially as women).

But also, and this is crucial, put yourself first knowing that you deserve it. Not because you've earned it, but simply because you *exist*. Realize that you are worthy of that prioritization of your time and energy. You need to put yourself first because nobody else will—and that goes for all of us. Self-love is the path to all love, and it sets the bar for every relationship in your life.

Shining the light of care and attention inward might rub people the wrong way at first, and that's fine. It can be an adjustment for others when you aren't as responsive or accessible as you've been in the past, but you're just showing them what is acceptable.

You're also encouraged to figure out what brings you joy and commit to allowing it into your life consistently, without guilt. Get a pillowcase that your face loves sleeping on. Buy a candle with a scent that makes you swoon. Go for a walk with your favorite podcast.

I have a client with young kids, and she does her groceries on the weekend while her husband is home with the kids. She always tells him she'll be back thirty minutes later than necessary so she can grab a coffee and read her book, enjoying a few moments of uninterrupted, caffeinated bliss.

Everyone benefits from remembering that self-care is never selfish—it's self-preservation. Once you get some practice and see the positive effects that come from prioritizing yourself, it gets easier to do (you'll also be setting a great example for your family—especially kids—and friends).

When your output is greater than the input, it's like being on an airplane when the cabin pressure drops. Everyone's told to put on their own mask before helping others, but here you are, belly-crawling up the aisle to help the flight attendants with theirs.

The Four of Wands is telling you to put your own damn mask on.

FIVE OF WANDS

*The Five of Wands is ready to serve a
big cup of shut up.*

It's a rare Wands card that doesn't have a happy, inspiring message. The Five of Wands is one of those cards, featuring a bunch of dudes beating the crap out of each other.

This is a feisty card of misunderstandings, competition, pettiness, bickering, and passive aggressiveness. It's everyone getting on your last nerve, like a long car ride with cranky kids. It's the prickly energy that stems from miscommunication and misunderstandings, like receiving a sarcastic text that doesn't translate well, so you reply with a snarky tone, and suddenly you're in a whole kerfuffle based on nothing.

Thankfully, this isn't long-term stuff you can't handle. The Five of Wands is like a fly buzzing around your head as you fall asleep: It's super annoying, but not particularly dangerous. When Bob won't stop talking in the meeting that could've been an email, and you want to flip the boardroom table like a Real Housewife? That's the Five of Wands in action.

When I was pregnant with my son, I consumed at least six meals a day because the act of eating was the only cure for my unrelenting nausea. If meals were missed or cravings neglected, there would be Serious Consequences.

I worked in downtown Toronto during this time, with an endless supply of fast food just an elevator ride away. One morning, shortly after consuming my post-breakfast brunch, I heard a Taco Bell commercial on the radio and was immediately consumed with fierce cravings: I needed a burrito, and I needed it twenty minutes ago.

I grabbed my coworker (Hi, Mitzi!) to hit up the nearest Taco Bell, which was also the jankiest one in the city. As we approached, I could see the rolling security gate still in place, despite it being ten minutes past opening. I rapped my knuckles on the glass and added a hopeful "Hello? Anybody there?" to no avail.

By now I was openly salivating, and Mitzi knew better than to suggest we forego our chimichangas. "HELLLOOO!" I yelled, wrapping my fingers around the grill of the metal gate and banging the glass, like a toddler who missed her nap. "IT'S TIME TO OPEN BECAUSE PEOPLE ARE HUNGRY!" My unhinged harassment morphed into tears of frustration, and Mitzi consoled me as I shuffled back to the food court near our office.

To this day, if someone has a meltdown—I mean a serious lose-your-shit moment—it is referred to by a certain friend group as "going Taco Bell." I haven't gone truly Taco Bell since that first time with Mitzi, but I've witnessed many such freak-outs over the years (usually involving toddlers).

The power of other cards might be stronger, but the volume on the Five of Wands is jacked to the max. Don't let its volatile vibe distract you, even if it's a crazy pregnant lady going ballistic for a burrito.

SIX OF WANDS

The Six of Wands is giving you a standing ovation.

I love getting this card because it indicates external validation for your efforts, which often shows up as a raise, promotion, or job offer. But these kudos can go beyond career. Featuring a hero returning from battle, the Six of Wands is getting thrown a parade because he's so fabulous.

Whether you're in school, at home with kids, or retired, this card reflects putting yourself out there to be truly seen and being celebrated for who you are and what you're bringing to the table.

This acclaim can show up as a big bag of money, an award, or a pat on the back, but regardless of how it is communicated, know that it's well-deserved recognition and success, so enjoy it.

SEVEN OF WANDS

The Seven of Wands rises above the bullshit.

This is another tricky card, with sticks flying up to attack this guy, but he's okay because he has literally risen above the fray. The Seven of Wands needs you to do the same, figuratively.

Don't let people push your buttons to get you to engage, and resist the urge to sink to their level. Otherwise, they'll get their hooks in you and drag you down into that low-vibe energy. Instead, channel your inner Zen and be the bigger person. Take the high road to avoid getting stuck in the muck, outnumbered with a target on *your* back.

The Seven of Wands asks for maturity on your part, which can be difficult when you're surrounded by a bunch of ding-a-lings. There is, however, an infinitesimal moment between when you receive something and when you respond or react, and you can draw that moment out and defuse it by thinking to yourself: *Interesting point of view.*

If a coworker gives you a pointed once-over and asks "What did you do to your hair?" instead of a snarky retort, try thinking quietly to yourself, *Interesting point of view.* This little trick can help you disconnect from a charged moment, giving you a buffer between what was said and your reaction to it. It reminds you that just because someone says something doesn't mean it's true: It's an opinion, and our opinions can be different. But you have to keep this technique to yourself rather than say it out loud, because there's often a subtext that says *Interesting point of view, dumbass.*

The opinions of others aren't your business, and statements aren't always facts. The Seven of Wands is a gentle reminder that sometimes you have to turn the other cheek and be the bigger person. Resist getting dragged into the drama, no matter how tempted you might be. This may not feel satisfying in the moment, but it will pay off in the long run.

EIGHT OF WANDS

Eight of Wands takes you from dormant to dynamic.

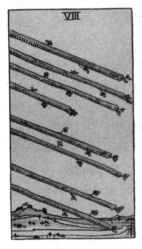

The Eight of Wands is all about communication, with sudden bursts of activity or fast-moving energy. These Wands were in a pile doing nothing until a catalyst of some sort caused them to go shooting through the air.

This card tells you that something you think is never going to happen will suddenly get a kick start, seemingly out of nowhere, and start progressing in a positive direction.

It could be travel or a literal move, but things will get moving in whatever area of life (relationships, work, health, etc.) has seemed stuck. What was once stagnant will be ignited, so get ready.

NINE OF WANDS

Nine of Wands is your biggest cheerleader.

The Nine of Wands is barely hanging on, like Rocky in the final round: battered and bruised, but ready to keep fighting. This card has a defensive and protective energy. It reassures you that you have the willpower and integrity that's needed to meet the moment you're in.

It's also a card of perseverance, reminding you that when things get tough, you can do tough stuff: You've had to in the past, you'll have to in the future, and you can do it now. The Nine of Wands encourages you to never give up—on yourself. Keep pushing because you're so close to getting there (wherever *there* is).

The vibe of this card is like getting to the end of a marathon, when runners start to fall apart as they approach the end, and the cheering bystanders propel them across the finish line. That's how the Nine of Wands is supporting you with this message: *You're so close! Don't give up! You're almost there!*

TEN OF WANDS

The Ten of Wands eases your burdens.

This dude has been lugging around a heavy load for a long time, but his destination is finally coming into view.

The Ten of Wands reassures you that a weight you've been carrying—it could be financial, physical, spiritual, mental, emotional, or a combination—will soon be lifted.

It can show up in your job, family, health, or any other area of life; when that burden is lifted, you'll finally be able to take a full breath and the relief will be palpable. It's in your sights. Keep pushing ahead—you're almost there.

TAROT TIP: When the Ten of Wands shows up in a reading, it can be helpful to pull another card for insight around what can be done to facilitate the easing of burdens. This is how tarot often operates—by offering an enticing or unburdening card along with one telling you how to make it happen (or not screw it up). For this reason, I might also pull a clarifying card alongside the Six of Wands or Page of Wands.

PAGE OF WANDS

The Page of Wands brings good news.

For some, the Page of Wands conveys motivated, lively energy. For others, it represents an enthusiastic young tween or someone in an assistant role. In my readings, the Page of Wands has a singular and wonderful meaning: Good news is coming your way.

It might be about a job offer, passing grade, positive health results, financial settlement, or any other area of your life. This card can't tell you when it's coming or what it looks like—that kind of prediction is veering into fortune-telling territory—it's more like an approaching weather system that's bringing good news along with it.

KNIGHT OF WANDS

*The Knight of Wands is inviting you
to the party that is your life.*

This figure is up for anything, with an essence that is energetic, passionate, lustful, and impulsive. Traditionally, this card represents travel or positive messages. For me, the Knight of Wands is urging you to live your life from a place of *YES!* as opposed to *Not now ... maybe later ... can't do it ...*

Ask for—and be open to receiving—opportunities for adventure, excitement, play, joy, lightness, and fun. Adventure can be climbing Mount Everest or trying Peruvian food for the first time. Maybe it's moving abroad or signing up for a workshop.

It's stretching out of your comfort zone in ways that feel awkward and a little scary. But it's not poop-your-pants terror—it's more like a-little-pee-running-down-your-leg excitement. This card is unlocking the door to *YES!* so you can have a little more fun with your life.

You know how little kids get giddy to roll down a hill? I'm not suggesting you go rolling down a hill (unless you want to), but maybe try looking at life through a lens of exuberance more often. Say *YES!* to finding more joy in the little things. And when those opportunities to say *YES!* show up in your life—and they will if you're open to it—don't turn your back on them because you need to do laundry because nobody gets to their last day wishing they'd done more laundry.

Get comfortable choosing desire over duty. Your life is the party of the year—you need to RSVP before it's too late.

QUEEN OF WANDS

The Queen of Wands is stepping into her potential (and so are you).

This Queen's warm, vibrant personality is irresistible because she's figured out her purpose and is living her best life—as the best version of herself. The Queen of Wands is incredibly self-assured and passionate about life, with a vibe that announces to the world *Hi, I'm here. You're welcome.*

The Queen of Wands is a natural leader, an enthusiastic multitasker sought out for her advice and assistance. She is a beacon, guiding you along the path to your enlightenment. The Queens of tarot represent actual people in my readings, and usually it's you, especially with the Queen of Wands because she's validating the idea that you're on the path to becoming the highest version of yourself—and also that you must keep going because there's still work to be done.

TAROT TIP: I always pull at least one more card with any Queen or King to learn more about how this energy can be embodied or what needs to be known about this person.

KING OF WANDS

> In the school of life,
> this is your prom king.

The King of Wands is a natural leader, with the strategic vision of a born entrepreneur. He's fun-loving, collaborative, and the life of the party—always up for a good time. He has the upbeat energy of a motivational speaker or actor, very comfortable in the spotlight.

At his best, this King is honest, loyal, engaging, and charismatic. On the other end of the spectrum, the King of Wands can struggle to follow through on his big ideas, coming off less as a visionary leader and more like a sleazy salesman pitching you an off-brand Rolex from the trunk of his car.

The King of Wands can symbolize the characteristics of his suit in an actual person, regardless of gender or sexual orientation, so he could easily be you. He can also be a placeholder for your partner, son, boss, friend, teacher, dad, or someone else. He might be the love of your life or the Realtor you hire in three months to sell your condo—don't worry too much about naming Kings because they often just give context to the cards around them.

∞

The bold, exciting energy of Wands is intoxicating. Aside from a couple of cranky cards (hi, Five of Wands), they're full of inspiration, potential, and adventure. When Wands show up in your reading, more often than not you're in for a good time.

CHAPTER 11

∞

Bottoms Up
(Cups)

Cups are all about matters of the heart. They're romantic, vibrant cards focused on feelings, creativity, intuition, and relationships. While Cups deal with the full range of emotions, they can also reflect other forms of abundance (and the work required to welcome more of that energy into your life). Cups represent the season of summer, the element of water, and the signs of Cancer, Scorpio, and Pisces.

ACE OF CUPS

The Ace of Cups is love in all forms.

Aces are the strongest card in a suit because they haven't been divided, and the Ace of Cups is the purest form of love. It can refer to romantic love or the love between parent and child, good friends, or siblings, or even love for yourself. It represents very honest, open, and genuine adoration.

You need to ensure that you're open to giving this love and, more importantly, receiving it. For now, just know that your life is overflowing with an abundance of love in all forms from a multitude of sources—even if you can't quite see it.

TWO OF CUPS

The Two of Cups rethinks the role of the soulmate.

In conventional tarot imagery, this looks like a traditional husband and wife. And while the familiar and undeniable soulmate energy of this card can be romantic, it also applies to friends, family, colleagues, or anyone else giving you a *This-ain't-our-first-time-at-the-rodeo* vibe.

In my readings, the Two of Cups wants you to reconsider the role of these sacred connections (and yes, we all have *many* soulmates) because it's not the lovey-dovey stuff that matters most. These people are in your life because class is in session—you're here to teach each other, be taught by each other, and hold up a mirror to each other. Sometimes it's like a cute course at your local community center, while other times it's more like a double PhD. Whether your connection lasts forty minutes or forty years, make no mistake—your souls are on an assignment together. There is important work to be done.

My readings are mostly forward-facing, but this is one of those cards (along with The Tower, The Star, and Six of Cups) that can help you view the past through a new lens, allowing you to reframe your experience and move forward unencumbered. This work you are doing with your soulmate (and it *is* work) is as essential, meaningful, and intimate as it is complicated, messy, and difficult.

I met two of my soulmates on the same day at a ballroom dance class I took at university. I felt an instant connection between myself and two of the four fellas in attendance. One of them, let's call him Joe, was an aspiring doctor, sometimes actor, and total goofball. We immediately started joking around and got in trouble for laughing during the foxtrot. The other, we'll call him Steve, was a charismatic and mysterious Air Force pilot trainee. We barely spoke, but the electricity between us was so palpable that, after one waltz, I wanted to climb him like a tree. Guess which one became a lifelong friend while the other is a cautionary tale?

Joe was my confidant, cheerleader, and sounding board. He taught me how to have fun and not take myself too seriously; I taught him how to flirt with women and dress himself. Steve was a torrid love affair full of drama, heartache, and chaos—I followed him to Moose Jaw, Saskatchewan (it was even worse than it sounds), and fled six months later after he knocked up a one-night stand. Both were my soulmates and I'm grateful for each of them because they taught me about the world and, most importantly, myself.

Your worst enemy can be your soulmate (that's where some of the juiciest growth can occur), and these fellow teachers and students can be people you've known your entire life or someone you met last week. It may take a minute to realize the reason for these connections, but trust that you will experience a moment of clarity at some point. Reframing your relationships is liberating. It's not always fun, but it's very necessary work.

THREE OF CUPS

The Three of Cups invites you to raise a glass.

This is a fabulous card of celebration in all forms. It's getting together with your nearest and dearest to raise a glass.

The Three of Cups is an opportunity to toast yourself and others—it can be a special occasion, an accomplishment, or making it through a tough time. Regardless of the *why*, this card encourages you to celebrate because you deserve it.

TAROT TIP: As mentioned earlier, I typically pull another card with this one to get insight on how this energy can be facilitated with as much speed, grace, and ease as possible.

FOUR OF CUPS

*The Four of Cups is a gentle kick in
the ass to be more present.*

Despite having those cups (which represent love and abundance) right in front of him, this person is pouting under a tree. He's too bored, confused, apathetic, or distracted to pay attention and appreciate what's already there before him.

The Four of Cups warns you to not live in the past, marinating in regret. But don't focus on a future that hasn't happened yet either because that's anxiety. Instead, live in the *now*.

Avoid the dissatisfaction that comes with "grass is always greener" thinking. And stay away from the trap of if-then thinking, which demands perfect conditions before you can fulfill the deal you've made with yourself (*If I lose twenty pounds, then I'll find love . . . If I had a different job, then I'd be happy . . .*). Getting stuck in this energy can lead to an uninspired life.

Lamenting the past and fantasizing about the future get you nowhere; this mindset lets you escape feeling and dealing with the present, keeping you stuck. You could waste years of your life daydreaming, which is just fantasy fueled by doubt. This is what happens when you don't believe in yourself: Time slips away and life passes you by as you seek to ignore the seemingly unbearable.

Be more in the moment so you don't miss the opportunities and guidance that are coming your way. Those tickling little feathers of awareness can become bricks to the face if we ignore them long enough.

The Four of Cups is the second cranky grandpa card (the first one was Justice) that urges you to get up and get going.

FIVE OF CUPS

The Five of Cups is urging you to stop the pity party.

The Five of Cups commonly depicts regret, grief, and disappointment, as evidenced by the dude crying over what has been spilled. He's being called to look at life from a more glass-half-full perspective because some of those cups are upright.

In my readings, this card goes even further to remind you that every bad relationship, situation, or experience contains a takeaway. It may not be a gift or lesson (let's not get carried away), but even if your only takeaway is realizing what you don't want, or getting clear on boundaries thanks to your dirtbag ex, these are valuable insights!

We often have to dig through the rubble to get the rubies, and sometimes it's fifty tons of crap to get a dinky little rock, but that's sort of the point. When things are falling apart, leaving you feeling helpless and hopeless, remember that there will usually be a moment down the road when you'll have a better understanding. It might take ten minutes or ten years, but clarity will come eventually (we usually want it in advance rather than in retrospect, but that's not how it works).

I don't think everything happens for a reason—I think that's dumb—but I strongly believe that you can take something from everything that happens. Your wounds may become wisdom that lights the path for others on their healing journey. Whatever happened, happened—that won't change. But it is only one part of your story, not *the* story. In the depths of loss and discomfort you find out who you really are. No experience is wasted... ever.

SIX OF CUPS

*The Six of Cups is ready to
Burn Your Sh*t.*

Traditionally, this card symbolizes nostalgia and naivety. In my readings, it highlights too much focus on the past. You can't move forward when you're looking over your shoulder, and the Six of Cups invites you to release resentments, grudges, or things you just haven't been able to move past. Let go of old stories you've been telling yourself about how things are supposed to be. Ditch the unrealistic expectations you have of everyone, including yourself.

Otherwise, it's like you're trudging along the beach, lugging a huge sack of rocks, looking for more heavy rocks to add to your load. These rocks are the grievances, hurts, and regrets that serve no purpose aside from weighing you down and holding you back.

The Six of Cups needs you to drop that sack full of energetic crap so you can discover your purpose and step into your potential. Make sure you feel your feelings because if you try to numb, ignore, or deny them—rather than facing, processing, and releasing them—they'll settle in and become emotions, which are a lot stickier.

Feelings show up fast, and we can identify them in the moment because they're a conscious experience. Emotions are deeper because they originate as sensations in the body and manifest in the unconscious mind, leading to limiting beliefs. Think of your emotions as the engine of a car, while the feelings are the frame—both are essential, but the power comes from the engine. Not taking the time to understand the depths of your emotions or express your feelings can be destructive on a physical, emotional, and spiritual level.

Instead of reliving every crappy thing that ever happened to you, acknowledge your past as just one part of your story. When you feel it, you can heal it. Have an ugly cry if you feel the urge. Punch a pillow. Scream in a closet. See a therapist. Go for a run. Write a poem. Do what you need to do in whatever time it takes. Be in your feelings so you can process them, metabolize them, and release them. You're not breaking down—you're breaking open.

Consider the outdated ideas and identities you're holding on to that no longer apply. The achievements of your past don't prove the worth of your present (or potential of your future), so stop clinging to artifacts.

Sometimes, a ritual is required to help you energetically let go of the beliefs, people, or circumstances that are holding you back—which is the perfect opportunity to Burn Your Sh*t. I've done Full Moon fire ceremonies for decades, leading groups in person and online, and I know how powerful and cathartic release rituals can be. "Burn Your Sh*t" is what I call my monthly gathering on Instagram Live, where our virtual coven sets fire to the past.

The Moon is our emotional compass; it represents the sacred feminine and intuition. A Full Moon ritual can help release barriers you may not even be aware of and allow your mind, body, and spirit to heal. Because a Full Moon is a supercharged time of the month where energy peaks and then releases, it brings things to the surface that need to go so you can move forward unburdened.

Before you go digging out someone's old sweater or lugging furniture into the backyard, be aware that the ritual is not about burning actual objects—it's much more powerful. You're releasing the limiting beliefs, negative self-talk, and any other funky mojo that's keeping you from reaching your potential and discovering your purpose. You need to set fire to all of the energetic crap that's holding you back to make space for the excellent energy coming your way. If you're new to rituals, here is an overview to get you started (or I'll see you on Instagram Live):

> Full Moon rituals can happen on your own, or you can gather some friends to make it a little coven. You can be outside or inside, but if you're indoors, make sure you're in a well-ventilated area. You'll need a pen, some slips of paper, a bowl (not plastic!), a lighter or matches, and a glass of water. Take a moment to close your eyes and ground yourself with a few deep breaths.
>
> Think about what (or who) is holding you back from stepping into your power and discovering your purpose. Consider what you need to release in order to reach your potential. What is keeping you from bravely speaking your truth? It can be attitudes, emotions, illness, debt, grudges, addictions, or habits. Is it a toxic relationship? Are limiting beliefs getting in your way? Is it where you're living? Not believing you're lovable? Not knowing your worth? Is it a specific job or how you perceive money? Is it how you look at your body?
>
> Focus on what comes to mind—what is stopping you from being unapologetically, authentically *you*? Notice what comes up, and trust your intuition. Are you ready to write a eulogy to a past relationship? Release the unfounded fears that were foisted upon you as a child? Leave the job that depletes your spirit? You may have a laundry list of things to release or one main thing that is blocking you, but trust what comes to mind.
>
> Now, open your eyes, pick up your pen, and write down the following words: *I now choose to release...* Then write what

came up for you on separate slips of paper. Don't do it all on one page; give each item the respect and ceremony it deserves. As you light each piece of paper on fire, speak each statement aloud and follow it up with *And so it is* at the end.

Here are some examples:

I now choose to release the resentment I feel toward this person . . .
　light the paper on fire over your bowl . . . *And so it is.*
I now choose to release the compulsion and expectation I feel to live my life for my parents . . . *light the paper on fire over your bowl* . . . *And so it is.*
I now choose to release the blocks, either conscious or unconscious, that are keeping me from moving forward with my business . . . *light the paper on fire over your bowl* . . . *And so it is.*

Take a deep breath and focus on those words burning. Some papers may go up in a whoosh while others are a bit more stubborn to burn. Notice how it feels to see them disappear before your eyes. You may find yourself sighing, there might be tears, or your stomach could start gurgling like crazy—these are all signs of shifting energy. You are reclaiming your power and stepping into your story as the author rather than a passive reader.

Transform every bit of paper into ash, and when you're done, add water to the container before dumping it all in your garden, down a sewer grate, in a park, on your lawn, or even down your toilet. By doing this, you've brought the four elements of nature into play: fire (the most transformative); water (the most purifying); air (the engine that makes it go); and earth (where everything is put to rest).

Full Moons give this ritual a bit of extra juice by harnessing that lunar energy, but you can Burn Your Sh*t on a random

Tuesday morning if you feel inspired—it still works. If your living situation doesn't allow for fire rituals, ripping up the paper and flushing it (don't clog your pipes!), burying it outside, or dumping it in the trash can also be very cathartic.

The Six of Cups tells you to let your past inform you, not define you. We all hold the capacity to adapt, evolve, and heal. It's never too late to become the person you're meant to be.

SEVEN OF CUPS

The Seven of Cups needs you to decide.

Being decisive can be difficult when you're overwhelmed with options, but the Seven of Cups doesn't want you falling into the trap of paralysis by analysis. Don't put off making a decision because you're hoping something better will come along, and avoid playing possibilities against each other to see what happens, because you'll find yourself with no options left at all.

Indecision doesn't delay the possibility of failure—it ensures it.

Much like its Major Arcana counterpart, The Chariot, this card reminds you not to let logic, emotion, or intuition hijack your decision-making process. Instead, give your head, heart, and gut an equal voice. Unlike The Chariot, the ramifications of these choices aren't as heavy, but they also can't be ignored. (If you get both cards in a reading, pay extra attention to the head-heart-gut connection.)

Imagine being in school and having to choose between two people who like you. You go off with your friends to make a pros-and-cons list for each candidate and while you're busy trying to decide, the whole thing falls apart. When it comes to making the right decision, the key is to be decisive.

EIGHT OF CUPS

The Eight of Cups is directing you to ditch the dead weight.

At first glance, this perfectly balanced stack of shiny golden cups would impress anybody. But they're not enough for the figure who's leaving them behind. The Eight of Cups shows how disillusioned he is, leaving him no choice but to turn his back and search for something more satisfying.

The Moon represents the fears, doubts, and insecurities that show up when we're faced with the unknown. It's hard to leave something (or someone) behind that you know isn't right because at least it's familiar. People often convince themselves to settle for less when it's comfortable or easy, desperately hoping that it will be enough (spoiler: It will not). The good news? On the other side of that mountain it's all sunshine, rainbows, and puppies. He's just not there yet. He's at the scary point in his journey, turning his back on what's known in search of something that's true.

It's okay to leave behind what isn't working for you and look for something different. This can include where you're living or working, the car you drive, relationships or friendships, whether you eat dairy, how you deal with money or conflict, religious or political views . . . anything in your life that isn't serving you is not *for* you.

This doesn't mean marching into work tomorrow and throwing

down your resignation, but you could update your résumé to get some momentum going in a different direction. You might take a more nuanced approach, such as rethinking how you deal with your boss, rather than walking away from the job altogether. Maybe it's realizing that if you met your longtime friend in the street, you wouldn't even want to grab a coffee, so why are you wasting each other's time?

Those beautiful cups that look perfect on paper are nothing more than spray-painted tin. The surface may shimmer, but underneath it's just a cheap knockoff wrapped in gold foil.

Whether it's tangible objects, relationships, situations, or beliefs, it's in your best interest to let go of anything out of alignment—before the pain of staying outweighs the pain of leaving.

NINE OF CUPS

The Nine of Cups attracts abundance with gratitude.

The Nine of Cups has been one of my favorite cards since day one. This card is all about dreams coming true and wishes being granted. Having your needs met and desires fulfilled.

Like a genie in a bottle, the Nine of Cups is seated in satisfaction. He is perfectly content—a state far different from fleeting happiness, which comes and goes. Contentment doesn't mean settling into complacency. Being content is a deep intrinsic knowing that not only do you *have* enough, but you *are* enough.

And isn't that the goal?

I recently threw out four very large, very expensive candles that

I bought almost thirty years ago. For over a quarter century, I have carefully wrapped and packed these candles before moving them across the country, only to unpack and display them in several different homes without lighting a single one.

Were there times I could have held a match to at least one of these pricey fucking candles? Of course! But I always hesitated, thinking I'd save them for a special occasion. I got married, birthed two babies, raised them, sent one off to college, got divorced, and navigated menopause—and through it all, the time never seemed right.

So what changed? Why did I suddenly decide to trash these (still unlit) candles? In a word: COVID. As our worlds started to shrink and we faced immeasurable loss, we were forced to face our mortality as we reconsidered what "enough" looked like.

The tarot readings I gave during this time had a common theme: *What the fuck am I doing with my life?* My clients were forced to seek clarity around the alignment of their values and beliefs with who they were and how they were living. From romantic relationships and careers to physical health and spiritual beliefs—everything was up for evaluation. For me, it was candles.

As my world got smaller, my life expanded. I took pleasure in little moments that would normally go unnoticed. I appreciated that I could be content without being stagnant. My creativity soared, and I was far more productive because I was fueled by flow rather than fear. I refused to be the woman who died surrounded by relics she'd been too scared to enjoy while she was alive. I threw out those ancient candles because they represented an old way of thinking (and being).

As I gained gratitude for the moment I was in, the doors to abundance opened. I don't mean the usual gratitude platitudes about a healthy family or the roof over your head (although those are worthy of endless thanks). I'm talking about the everyday stuff we often take for granted. It turns out abundance was there all along—I just needed to finally acknowledge it.

There's a saying that "the braver you are, the luckier you get." I'd argue that the more grateful and content you are, the less you need to rely on luck. Gratitude for what is creates space for what could be.

So please, for the love of Goddess, light the expensive candle. Savor the crème brûlée cheesecake. Order the sparkly shoes. Stop waiting for special occasions because—spoiler alert—life is the special occasion.

TEN OF CUPS

The Ten of Cups is family in all forms.

Although the Ten of Cups looks like the perfect family unit with two kids and a minivan, it's really a card of connections.

You have a family of origin and also your chosen family—those people with whom you share a deep bond of familiarity in your soul (and there can definitely be some overlap between the two). This card reminds you of the depth and strength of connections in your life. Like tree roots in a rainforest, they grow deeper and spread wider than you may realize. These roots often hold us up until we're steady enough to support ourselves.

Don't hesitate to lean on these connections—ask for assistance, a shoulder to cry on, or a second opinion. Think about your reaction when a friend calls you in need; you rush to offer your support because helping others feels so good. The Ten of Cups wants you to give the people in your life that same gift by letting *them* help *you*. We often hesitate to reach out, thinking we'll be a burden, but *everyone* feels better when we allow those moments of connection. This card is pointing out that family comes in many forms, and we're not meant to do it all alone, so don't bother.

Also make sure to leverage the connections in your life when necessary. Ask if anyone knows someone who knows someone who can help you; your network is more extensive than you realize.

In times of crisis, often the last thing we want is to trouble others, but that's exactly when we need to reach out. Lean on your support network as needed—your family is there, waiting for the call.

PAGE OF CUPS

The Page of Cups knows that vulnerability is your superpower.

The Page of Cups card traditionally symbolizes a younger person or creative energy, but my interpretation goes much deeper and in a slightly different direction. The vulnerability of this card is calling on you to rediscover the tender essence of who you are—nurturing the tiny ember of your true self that may have been smothered when you were young. In doing so, you'll encounter the path you're meant to travel.

The Page of Cups urges you to become more available, accessible, and vulnerable with your heart because you've built walls around it. These walls served their purpose very well, but they're no longer needed—it's time to tear them down.

There's a bunch of woo woo stuff you can do, like a heart chakra meditation or carrying a rose quartz crystal in your bra, but from a more practical point of view, you're being called to live with an open heart. Being wholehearted means saying how you feel with no strings attached or doing something for someone without expecting anything in return. It's being unapologetically, authentically yourself.

This doesn't mean abandoning boundaries and flinging yourself open like Walmart on Black Friday. But for the people who've earned a place in your heart, it's safe to let those walls come down so you can open up and be vulnerable. The Page of Cups recognizes that vulnerability is a place of power, strength, and growth rather than shame, weakness, or fear.

I call this the Brené Brown card because she is a social scientist who specializes in the study of vulnerability and shame, especially as it applies to leadership. Her Netflix special, *The Call to Courage*, extrapolates the essence of this card, so watching it is the homework I offer clients who have it show up in a reading. She'll help you understand that vulnerability isn't a liability—it's your superpower.

You're being called upon to be brave so you can step fully into your life. It's time to say how you feel and be who you are without fear of repercussions. Embrace vulnerability as a strength rather than a weakness. Have the courage to be yourself, knowing that it's enough because you're enough—just as you are.

KNIGHT OF CUPS

The Knight of Cups is an offering of heart and soul.

Traditionally seen as the romantic knight in shining armor on an endless quest for beauty and truth, the Knight of Cups can represent a proposal of marriage, or a declaration of love and adoration.

For me, this card can also represent a job, side hustle, or hobby that you pour your passion into. This could include entrepreneurs, creatives, or those in healthcare and education, but it applies to anyone deeply passionate about their work.

Whether it's a partner or fling, vocation or passion project, the Knight of Cups is all love, all the time.

TAROT TIP: This is another card I like to supplement with an additional one because on its own, it doesn't provide much insight. The Knight of Cups can offer some context, but an extra card typically delivers the message or call to action.

QUEEN OF CUPS

*The Queen of Cups
feels everything.*

This Queen rules the realm of feelings. Sometimes, the ethereal Queen of Cups may not seem stable because she experiences every emotion to the extreme, but it's because she's living life in her imagination and intuition.

Despite being the Queen of emotions, in my readings she hasn't mastered matters of the heart. She's typically *really* happy, *really* depressed, *really* excited, *really* confused . . . she's feeling *all* the things.

As with the other Queens, this card isn't necessarily saying that her attributes are you or the person you're reading, but her characteristics are at the forefront in relation to the cards around her or where she's placed in the spread.

This Queen's heart space is heightened and that energy is being brought out by everything that's happening around her. She has Taylor Swift on repeat and her freezer stocked with Ben & Jerry's just in case she needs it (spoiler: She's gonna need it).

We don't want to suppress or ignore our feelings; the Queen of Cups simply highlights her heart-centered presence. She's a reminder to be gentle with yourself as you navigate emotional minefields. This awareness helps prevent you from getting caught in her sensitive undertow, shifting from feeling to wallowing. Feel deeply, but also, keep it moving.

KING OF CUPS

*The Zaddy game is strong
with King of Cups.*

While the Queen of Cups is all about her feelings—from empathetic caring to self-absorbed sulking—her King has emotional intelligence for days. A natural parent and partner, the King of Cups lives his life from a place of balance, creativity, and calm.

Chill and content, this swoon-worthy fella is very in touch with his feelings. Whether he's a sensitive artist or a banker with the soul of a poet, his sensitive side shines through. He can be a bit resistant to conflict and isn't outwardly gushy with his emotions, but the King of Cups is extremely affectionate and loving to the person holding the key to his heart.

I always envision this King sitting under a willow tree, beside a babbling brook with a sketch pad on his knee, creating with abandon. He's the King of intuition and imagination, but that doesn't mean he represents someone pursuing artistic endeavors—there are plenty of plumbers and lawyers who are very passionate and creative in their approach to work. At his best, the King of Cups symbolizes someone in a state of full flow. At his worst, his emotions can be so intense that he disconnects from them despite his yearning to marinate in all the feels.

Remember that Kings and Queens represent real people in your life, and they're more about characteristics than gender. Don't spend too much time trying to assign Kings to a specific person. The King of Cups could be a call to embody these attributes yourself, or he might be a placeholder for someone in your life, such as a romantic or business partner, child, boss, friend, or parent.

∞

How you react in your relationships and to the world around you is reflected in the Cups. Like water, their energy can flow as a gentle stream or crash as a torrential wave. Whether in moments of massive abundance or unbearable loss, Cups validate the fluidity of your feelings.

CHAPTER 12

∞

Pointy Parts
(Swords)

The suit of Swords deals with all matters of the mind. These action cards have a cool, calculated, and logical energy, often dealing with intellect and strategy. Being tested and facing conflict, both internal and external, are also recurring themes. This is a suit driven by thought over emotion, power over peace, and courage over charisma. Swords represent the element of air and the season of autumn, as well as the signs of Gemini, Libra, and Aquarius.

ACE OF SWORDS

The Ace of Swords is a call to arms.

Where the other cards offer a gentle nudge or glimpse of clarity, the triumphant Ace of Swords has a bossier vibe. For me, it is the most powerful card in the deck. The Ace of Swords is pushing you to be the protagonist of your story because it is uniquely yours to tell. This unstoppable energy challenges you to step fully into your life. No more living in the shadows and playing small.

The Ace of Swords demands that you shine as bright as you can, be as loud as you want, and take up all the space you need. And if people think you're being too loud or shining too bright, tell them to put on earmuffs and get some sunglasses, because their comfort is not your concern. The world needs you at maximum capacity, and that means showing up unapologetically in the world as your authentic self—knowing that it's enough because you are enough.

This card encourages you to own your choices and let your freak flag fly, without seeking anyone else's permission. Don't worry about pleasing everyone—that's impossible. Be yourself, and your people will be drawn to you like a magnet. Those who don't resonate with you will go off and find someone else, which is great because it creates more space for your people.

You're like a brilliantly colored peacock with its tail down, feathers tucked away, staying small and tiptoeing quietly to avoid drawing attention. The Ace of Swords says that's not going to cut it anymore. It's time to plant your feet at center stage, get those tail feathers out, and start shaking them like a Vegas showgirl.

Claim your space, use your voice, and own your truth—in all of its big, boisterous, beautiful glory.

TWO OF SWORDS

The Two of Swords is a self-imposed stalemate.

This figure is paralyzed by fear, sitting with her swords crossed in front of her, thinking *I'm safe. I don't know what I'm safe from, but at least I'm safe, so I'll just sit here and be safe from whatever might be unsafe.*

The Two of Swords is held back by worries, doubts, and insecurities, symbolized by the Moon. Her blindfold suggests she's unaware of what's keeping her stuck—and perhaps the details aren't hers to know—but the water around her is completely calm.

She could lower her guard, allow herself to be vulnerable, and remove the blindfold to discover there's nothing to fear. Then she could stand up and walk away. Or she could stay stuck indefinitely. The choice is hers to make.

It may seem like an easy choice, but so many of us stay stuck because we listen to our fears and doubts without questioning their merit. Those insurmountable obstacles are just tissue paper. Like The Devil, the good news with this card is that it's all in your head... unfortunately, that's also the bad news.

I often share personal stories in my readings that demonstrate a card's message in action, and the Two of Swords is a perfect example. Years ago, my accountant left me a voicemail asking to call him about an issue with my tax return. Every ounce of saliva evaporated in my mouth as my stomach dropped to the floor. Math was my weakest subject in school, and for a long time I got overwhelmed by the most basic bookkeeping.

Weeks passed without my returning my accountant's call. I was sick with worry, convinced I was about to be audited or arrested or maybe even deported (despite being born in Canada). After some deep breathing and a pep talk in the mirror, I finally called him back. "I need the year and model of your car so I can file your return," he said.

"That's it?" I asked, leaning on my kitchen counter for support. That was it. Hours spent worrying instead of sleeping, countless Tums taken, nails bitten to nubs . . . all because I hadn't picked up the phone to confirm what kind of car I drove. I still get a little queasy around tax season, but I try to remember that any issues are likely easy fixes. And, even in the worst-case scenario, I'm not getting deported.

The Two of Swords is here to reassure you that the anticipation you're feeling is much worse than the actuality and you're braver than you realize. Put down the swords, get uncomfortable, and do it anyway. You'll be so happy you did.

THREE OF SWORDS

The Three of Swords encourages a cathartic cry.

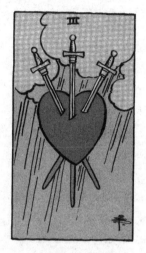

The Three of Swords can indicate heartbreak, but at its core, it signifies emotional fragility.

Things that would normally roll off your back are sticking and sticking (and sticking) until you can't take it anymore and finally fall apart. Minor obstacles feel major, and meltdowns are inevitable. You try to cope with overwhelming emotions through an ugly cry, a bath, or a drink (or all of the above), until you reemerge depleted and a little shaky, telling yourself and everyone around you that you're fine (but really, you're not).

This card reminds you that this storm is situational and circumstantial, like a rain cloud hanging over your head that feels like a tsunami, pouring down on you alone. You may not believe it at that moment, but you *can* handle it because it's not a dealbreaker—it's a mood.

As you navigate painful moments, make sure you're not mistaking rain clouds for tsunamis because that cloud will eventually dissipate on its own. Or you'll look up, see it for what it is (a funk), and step out from under it, leaving it behind.

Until then, go easy on yourself and your tender heart.

FOUR OF SWORDS

The Four of Swords needs you to strengthen your energetic core.

This guy isn't dead—he's just meditating like the Savasana corpse pose at the end of a yoga class. The Four of Swords advises you to replenish yourself energetically.

Some of the cards have similar themes, and this card is like a younger sibling of The Hermit. Both are asking you to do the same thing—unplug, step away from the to-do list and get quiet—but for different reasons. The Hermit wants you to disengage from your hectic life so you can access the guidance you're seeking. The Four of Swords needs you to top up your energy from the inside out. In order to shore up your energetic reserves, you have to go within. It doesn't have to be a five-hour yoga marathon, but some form of mindfulness that allows you to tap into that meditative zone will do wonders.

Try a quick breathing exercise when you wake up and before you go to bed.

> You can be sitting or lying down, but be intentional (e.g., not while you're making breakfast). Close your eyes and take five deep belly breaths, inhaling through your nose for a count of five, holding for a count of five, then exhaling for a count of eight. By breathing into your abdomen and exhaling longer than you inhale, you're activating your parasympathetic nervous system, which takes you from a state of fight-flight-freeze to a place of relax-rest-digest.

It allows you to transition from anxiety and panic into a more strategic, creative, and intuitive space.

With this intentional breathing, you're calming the lizard part of your brain and activating the smarty-pants part of your brain. Doing this practice—breathing in for five, holding for five, and breathing out for eight—twice a day can be a game-changer.

By stepping away from your busy life, even for a few breaths, you'll fortify your energetic core (and the Four of Swords implies that you'll need that strength).

FIVE OF SWORDS

The Five of Swords asks you to unclench.

My interpretation of the Five of Swords has evolved from the Tarot 101 definition (conflict and defeat) into something far more nuanced, resulting in my love-hate relationship with this card.

Here's the gross part: Something you want *so* badly—you've been banging your head against a wall trying to make happen—isn't happening. At least, not the way you *think* because there's too much clenching on your part. It's like a little kid clutching a bird to show his mom, yelling "Look at the bird! I LOVE THE BIRD SO MUCH!" until the bird's head pops off. That's happening energetically with you.

It's a very I'll-make-this-work-if-it-kills-me-because-I've-put-so-much-time-and-energy-into-it vibe. You need to strive for more of an if-it-works-it-works approach. It's time to unclench and stop trying to force things. Admitting that you can't do or get something (or someone) you want so desperately can be a hit to your ego, especially if you're the kind of person who says "Just give it to me so I know it will get done." The Five of Swords says, *Not this time, toots.*

Now for the delicious part: If you can put your ego aside and stop trying to dictate the outcome, you'll realize that whatever you were trying to force was actually blocking you from something much better. Or you'll end up getting what you wanted much faster, easier, cheaper, or with less pain.

Imagine putting an offer on your dream home after months of searching, then losing a bidding war. You go off in a snit and vow to rent for the rest of your life because the perfect house is impossible. Months later when the market softens, you can afford something that would've been way out of your price range, and you think, *Thank God I didn't get that first piece of garbage . . . look at this palace I'm in now!*

You see why it's the best and worst card? Unclenching can be incredibly difficult to do, but it makes things so much better in the long run. The Five of Swords isn't about giving up—it's surrendering the need to control the outcome, because, as the writer Elizabeth Gilbert says, you never really had control . . . you just had anxiety.

SIX OF SWORDS

The Six of Swords takes you from rough waters to smooth sailing.

Swords have a reputation for being scary or negative—and to be fair, there's one with a dead guy being impaled in a swamp (we'll get to him shortly). But not all swords are ominous. The Six of Swords is actually one of the most hopeful cards in the deck.

A mother and child are leaving behind the churning waters of a difficult situation, relationship, experience, etc. Although there are swords all around, none are touching them (unlike the dude in the swamp). A card with swords surrounding rather than stabbing a person symbolizes emotional distress. Other examples include the Two, Four, Five, Eight, and Nine of Swords (nobody said Swords were easy!). Yes, these six swords in the boat represent the anxiety and unease of tumultuous waters, but the figures are moving into a calm and steady future.

This message echoes the Ten of Wands, which focuses on easing burdens. There are seventy-eight cards in a tarot deck, and each one has a different story to tell, but some of the cards share similar threads or themes. When cards like these come together in a reading and I start sounding like a broken record, it's like the cards are shouting, *Are you listening? Did you hear it?! Do you get it?!?* This is the tarot equivalent of picking up a couple of trash-can lids like orchestral cymbals and clunking you on either side of the head with them.

Often the recurring messages have themes around taking action, healing within, or standing strong, but every so often a combination comes along, like Six of Swords and Ten of Wands, to give you a double dose of reassurance.

Whether it signifies literal travel or an inner journey, the Six of Swords transports you from a place of tension to one of tranquility.

TAROT TIP: Just like the Ten of Wands, this card offers an opportunity to pull an extra card—or two!—for additional insight on how you can facilitate the easing of these rough waters.

SEVEN OF SWORDS

The Seven of Swords needs you
to be selectively sneaky.

Traditionally, the Seven of Swords warns of potential treachery, deception, or betrayal of some sort. My readings flip the script a bit.

You're being reminded that there's a time and a place to be direct, assertive, and to the point. But in order to get what you want, sometimes you need to focus more on charm, subtlety, and diplomacy. Sometimes it can be more effective to slip through a side window than to barge through the front door. Maybe it's letting your bosses think your idea is their idea. Or getting group consensus by letting everyone speak and feel heard before bringing things around to where *you* want them to be.

This savvy card asks *you* to be manipulative, rather than being the target of dirty deeds. Not in a creepy or underhanded way; just strategic and tactical. It's being deliberate, not devious. And it's knowing which approach is required to get your way.

EIGHT OF SWORDS

The Eight of Swords has you stuck in a moment that feels like forever.

Nothing about the Eight of Swords looks encouraging This woman feels stuck, powerless, and isolated. The blindfold symbolizes her lack of awareness about what's keeping her trapped. Plus, all of those swords hanging around signify the stress that comes from feeling like you're out of options.

The Eight of Swords confirms that yes, there are circumstances beyond your control keeping things sticky; it's not all in your head. And her blindfold indicates that maybe it's not your business to know the details of why you're feeling so restricted (similar to the Two of Swords).

Thankfully, this card also gives you some much-needed perspective, reminding you that the easiest way through this unyielding energy is to let life unfold instead of trying to force it (which could tighten those ropes even more). This doesn't mean sitting back and doing nothing. The Eight of Swords is a daunting reminder that some situations need to resolve themselves organically.

Where you have agency in these circumstances is in your awareness of the story you're telling yourself—and whether you're making it a bigger deal in your mind. You can't worry something into existence, and your perception is something you can manage. In the moment, you may feel like it will never end, but it's just that—a moment. Try not to make mountains out of molehills as you wait for it to pass because it *will* pass—just not on your timeline.

It's like making a left turn against traffic during rush hour. The wait is endless and you're getting more frustrated by the second. And then someone slows down to let you in, or an oncoming car changes lanes to give you an opening. Or a gap opens in traffic because the light down the street changed. And you realize that you weren't really stuck there forever—it just felt that way.

People often want a tarot reading because they're feeling stuck—every part of life seems to be stalled, and they can't see a way forward. And you can usually do some work to get things moving, but you need to reflect on why moments of lethargy in your life might be necessary.

This happened with my client Jim, who was newly divorced and terrified of Tinder. He was counting down the months until his retirement from an unfulfilling job, and he felt like his life had fizzled to a standstill, leaving him frozen in amber.

I explained to Jim how we cycle through different seasons, just like the natural environment that surrounds us. Some seasons are lush and fruitful while others appear quieter and more desolate, but they're all essential to the cycle of life. In the harsh winter months, juicy work is happening beneath the surface to set the stage for spring. The same is true in our lives. Moments of apparent stillness or stagnation are often necessary because they allow us to replenish and heal as we prepare for what's to come.

Jim experienced this firsthand—he left his reading with homework that focused on burning his shit (Six of Cups), killing his inner critic (The Devil), and connecting to his intuition (The High Priestess). Jim needed this slower season in his outer world so he could dedicate himself to his inner world. Once he addressed his homework, things picked up in every area of his life.

Things won't stay stalled forever, and appreciating why it may be necessary can make life a little easier to endure.

NINE OF SWORDS

The Nine of Swords is freaking the fuck out.

This figure is inconsolable with worry—and the swords hovering in the background aren't helping. The Nine of Swords symbolizes the anxiety, fears, and racing mind that keep us up at night thinking, *Ohmygodohmygodohmygod*...

While the Eight of Swords reassures you that there are legit reasons for your stress, the Nine of Swords suggests that you're blowing things out of proportion. This person woke up from a bad dream and she's experiencing mental anguish rather than physical danger.

The Nine of Swords wants you to get your head out of your ass, which is hard to do when you're in the eye of the storm—because this storm is *your* storm. This card does not devalue or diminish your storm; it points out that the things keeping you awake and stressed at three o'clock in the morning rarely feel as scary at three o'clock in the afternoon. The middle-of-the-night spiral is real, but the threat behind it is never as dire in the light of day.

TEN OF SWORDS

The Ten of Swords is a necessary ending.

Nothing about this card looks good, and when it comes up in a reading, people usually react like they do with the Death card: panic, dread, and possible diarrhea. At first glance, it *is* a very ominous card because, let's face it, this dude is very dead. He's done. It's over.

The Ten of Swords looks scary and painful because even when we know something is ending, it can still suck because change can be difficult (see also: the Death card). But, similar to the Death card's ominous first impression, the Ten of Swords never refers to the physical death of any plant, pet, or person; instead, it offers a message that is ultimately positive.

The dawn breaking in the distance gives you a hint that something better is on the horizon. Whether it's where you live, the car you drive, your job, a relationship, or eating dairy—never forget that endings happen because something (or someone) new is waiting in the wings. Like with feng shui, you need to clear out the clutter so the good mojo can get in. Try to embrace the endings in your life, despite the discomfort they bring, because they're necessary. It's time. There was a reason and a season, and that season has now passed.

Similar to the Six of Cups and Eight of Cups, the Ten of Swords creates capacity for something greater. There is a welcome clarity of vision that comes with such a definitive conclusion (even if it feels horrible when it's happening).

Your job is to remember that these endings are always making space for better beginnings.

PAGE OF SWORDS

The Page of Swords tells you to zip it.

This card is traditionally associated with disappointing or delayed news, or an untrustworthy person. Modern interpretations lean more toward an abundance of energy (which just goes to show how fluid these definitions can be!). But in my readings it has always been a very clear directive: Shut your pie hole.

Notice how his sword is off to the side? He's keeping his cards close and being a bit coy, not revealing more than is necessary. The vibe is very *Show me yours and then I'll show you mine*...

The Page of Swords warns you not to share your business with people if it's not their business. Don't announce something prematurely or it could come back to bite you in the ass. It's not saying something bad will happen, but something bad *could* happen if you're too chatty.

Let's say you're in the lunchroom at work, talking about an internal posting for a job you desperately want that hasn't been announced yet. A coworker overhears you and applies for the new job before you've finished your yogurt. Or you're in line at the grocery store, talking on your phone about someone planning to leave her husband, and he's standing right behind you. Maybe you have a business idea that's so brilliant you can't resist bragging about it to your neighbors—and a month later one of them launches your million-dollar venture. Unfortunate outcomes like these can often be avoided with a little restraint.

Don't talk just to fill an uncomfortable silence. Try not to exaggerate the truth. Avoid gossip, and be wise with your words. Be careful about who you talk to and what you say. And when in doubt, zip it.

KNIGHT OF SWORDS

The Knight of Swords is barely contained chaos.

Most Knights are stable and dignified, but not the Knight of Swords—he's channeling some serious Tasmanian Devil vibes. Conventional meanings focus on an aggressive personality or divisive energy.

For me, this card's energy feels like getting on a log in the water and frantically struggling to climb on as it spins beneath your grasp. It's not necessarily negative, but it is overwhelming and uncomfortable.

As you try to navigate this tumultuous energy, not knowing what's ahead can feel unsettling because you're on edge and don't feel grounded. You don't have a handle on things the way you normally would, and while most tarot cards suggest a new perspective or different direction, the Knight of Swords just kind of stares back at you, as if to say *Yep—it's bonkers. What's your point?*

You can't control the storm swirling around you—it is what it is. What you *can* do is remember that things won't be like this for long and that you can handle it, even if you don't think you can. When you feel threatened by overwhelm, go for a walk, stand outside, or do something else to change the energy around you. If the chaos is something that must be endured, remember that the moment won't last forever—it just feels that way. You've got this.

QUEEN OF SWORDS

The Queen of Swords has no time for knuckleheads.

Every Queen has her own attributes, and when one shows up to represent you or another person in your life, the card is not saying that her personality is you, but elements of her character are being drawn out in relation to the cards around her. When it comes to the Queen of Swords, you may be called to step into her energy.

When you place all of the Queens side by side, you'll notice that the Queen of Swords stands out. The others are facing forward in a welcoming way, while this saber-bearing Queen is off to the side, ready to cut anyone who gets in her way. Her guarded demeanor may stem from loss, but regardless of how she got so cranky, this is a formidable Queen of intelligence, strategy, and action. She has an impressive business acumen and a spine of energetic steel. She's a champion for justice and equality, and her work ethic is unmatched.

The Queen of Swords isn't a bitch, but she can be bitchy (I resonate with this Queen *a lot*). Her vibe is *That's your answer? Are you serious?* She has zero tolerance for nonsense because she's got things to do—and she gets them done. Sometimes, we need to put on our big-girl pants and embrace her steely energy. On the other end of the spectrum, particularly in personal relationships, this Queen can get a bit rigid and abrasive, poking everyone around her like Edward Scissorhands in a balloon store.

When the Queen of Swords turns up in a reading, consider which version of her is showing up in your life and how you can step into her strengths while mitigating her more challenging aspects.

KING OF SWORDS

The King of Swords is
Mr. Smarty Pants.

This King is ethical and loyal, with an innate air of authority. He's able to appraise a situation without emotions getting in the way, allowing him to make strategic assessments based on facts. The King of Swords may not be the most adventurous or fun-loving royal dude (the King of Wands has that title locked down), but he's someone you can trust.

This intellectual powerhouse commands authority with his presence, but his shadow side can lean toward controlling. The King of Swords likes things done a certain way and can become a bit obsessive or critical as a result.

Like the other Kings, the King of Swords represents the attributes of a person more than gender, so it can be your partner, child, boss, friend, parent, or yourself. Don't worry too much about putting a name to him—he's often simply a placeholder for the characteristics mentioned above.

∞

Although the imagery of Swords can be intimidating, their calls to action and unvarnished observations are usually needed (if not always welcome). The energy of this suit is like a teacher who pushes you to do better and try harder because they know you have it in you.

CHAPTER 13

∞

Get That Bag
(Pentacles/Coins)

Coins are currency, and these cards often show up in readings with messages around money (making it, keeping it, and using it wisely). Many years ago, I replaced "pentacles" with "coins" in my tarot vernacular, which many people do for various reasons. I did it mostly because it's an easier word to say (which makes a difference when you do a lot of readings). In addition to finances and career, the practical, generous energy of this suit can also speak to stability, hard work, the material world, and prosperity in all areas of life. Their season is winter, and they represent the earth signs of Taurus, Virgo, and Capricorn.

ACE OF COINS

The Ace of Coins is amazing money mojo.

An ace is the strongest form of the suit because it hasn't been split up, and the Ace of Coins is tarot's most robust money card.

This card has Midas touch energy, turning everything into gold. The Ace of Coins can also indicate a gift, financial reward, or loan of some kind. With the Ace of Coins, there's a wave of good money vibes coming up behind you, and your job is to surf that wave instead of letting it wash over you.

If you're looking for a new job, raise, or promotion—things are looking good. If you're planning to invest, upgrade your education, or sell your home—now is the time. If you're waiting for a settlement or approval on a loan—the energy is excellent.

Getting the Ace of Coins in a reading doesn't guarantee you'll become a millionaire (it might just mean starting a side hustle on Etsy), but the energy behind it is incredible, and that's what matters. With this card, quality beats quantity—you're looking at top-tier, premium abundance—so make the most of this prosperous financial energy.

TWO OF COINS

The Two of Coins wants you to drop some plates.

This card has very busy energy, like the Knight of Swords, but more hectic than frantic. The Two of Coins is all about managing your time when there isn't enough of it. It's like you're spinning plates on sticks, rushing from one to the next as you try to keep them from crashing to the ground.

This balancing act requires hard work and fast feet. You can handle the hustle, but you need to understand that some of those spinning plates are like delicate china that requires your care and attention, while others are just cheap plastic crap from a dollar store. They might turn into good stuff down the road, but for now they're ninety-nine-cent specials, and it's time to let them go.

Don't spread yourself too thin, getting pulled in too many directions while trying to spin plates that can be dropped, delegated, or ignored. Whether it's folding the laundry (a personal fave to drop), trying to fit thirty hours of work into an eight-hour workday, or saying yes when you want to say no, make sure that you're not squandering your precious time.

Also consider how often you're frantically spinning Tupperware, treating it like Grandma's good china, because you feel a compulsion, pressure, or obligation to validate your contribution, value, or belonging. The Two of Coins wants you to understand how unnecessary that is—not to mention futile. Direct your energy with intention and streamline where possible to ensure that everyone benefits from your efforts—especially you.

THREE OF COINS

The Three of Coins tells you to elevate your life.

The guy on the bench is building a castle for the people who've come to check his progress and give him the go-ahead. The Three of Coins is giving you a similar sense of approval, showing that you have a strong base and it's time to take things to the next level.

Although it's a coin-specific card, this message can apply to your relationships, health, home, etc. Don't settle for the basement suite when you can have a high-rise. You might hesitate, thinking your foundation feels as shaky as a house of cards, ready to collapse at the first sign of stress. But the Three of Coins reassures you that it's more like cement encased in steel wrapped in titanium—it can withstand the weight of you upgrading your life.

Build upon what you have because your foundation is stronger than you realize. Don't let complacency keep you small. You're ready to step it up a notch—whatever *it* is.

FOUR OF COINS

*The Four of Coins reminds you,
"nothing ventured, nothing gained."*

This figure is standing with his coins perfectly balanced to avoid losing them—but he's not gaining either. He's holding his coins so tightly, obsessed with keeping them close, that he's missing opportunities to gather up. By focusing on not falling behind, he can't get ahead. He's stuck in a limbo of his own making, and to move past it, he needs to take a chance—and so do you.

These risks aren't physical (like jumping out of an airplane) or financial (don't take your rent to the casino). The Four of Coins is about the mental and emotional risk that comes with stretching beyond your comfort zone in ways that can feel scary, vulnerable, or awkward.

Taking a chance might mean putting yourself in a position of truly being seen (going to your first AA meeting), setting yourself up for potential failure (asking for a raise), or getting uncomfortable for a cause (showing up at a protest).

When you venture beyond your bubble of security, amazing things can happen. The rewards are greater than the risks so focus less on what's at stake and more on what's possible. It may feel like you're stuck in quicksand, but it's just a sandbox. Don't get trapped in mediocrity that's forged in a fear of the unknown.

Take a chance on yourself because you're worth it.

FIVE OF COINS

The Five of Coins needs you to
pay attention (or else).

I've always considered the Five of Coins to be misleading. There's a sense of poverty and desperation with the two people trudging barefoot through the snow instead of being inside with all the money, suggesting strain and anxiety. But the Five of Coins isn't financial hardship so much as a cautionary tale. These two missed out on the money because they weren't being careful and missed the door.

You're being asked to double-check everything and know exactly what you're getting into so it doesn't come back to bite you in the ass. The Five of Coins isn't saying something bad will happen, but something bad *could* happen if you aren't on top of things. Read the fine print on the contract before joining that new gym. Triple-check your résumé before sending it out. Make sure you haven't hit "reply all" on that email.

Being detail-oriented can apply to more than just your finances: Have a doctor check that funky mole; see if your friend has a fifth-floor walk-up and a waterbed before offering to help her move; ask if he's married before going on that date.

And if someone wants you to approve or sign up for something you don't understand, it's on them to explain it clearly so you can get it. If that doesn't work, bring in someone who *does* get it to advocate for you, like a lawyer, financial planner, or Realtor.

There's a fine line between meticulous and obsessive, so be careful not to cross from cautious to compulsive.

SIX OF COINS

*The Six of Coins wants you to know
your worth and invest accordingly.*

The Six of Coins anticipates some unexpected or owed money landing in your lap (it's never lottery tickets, so don't bother) and when money comes to you unexpectedly—maybe getting more back on your taxes than expected, paying off a debt early, or finding twenty bucks in your pocket—it's important not to be miserly and shove it under your bed forever, but also don't blow it on something frivolous. Instead, use it in a way that propels you to reach your potential.

It doesn't have to be an extravagant amount of money. Whether you're taking a class, getting a website designed for your side business, or just buying a lipstick that makes you feel fabulous, understand that you're worth the investment. If the idea of spending money on yourself feels reckless or wasteful, consider that your growth and success can put you in a position to share the wealth and help others.

For years I bought my underwear where I got my groceries (anything more seemed like a waste of money). At Christmas, I would always ask for useful presents the whole family would enjoy, like a blender. I was very bad at spending money on myself. All of that changed when I spent my fifty-second birthday getting my picture taken—naked.

Let's not get it twisted: The vibe was intentionally more Victoria's Secret than *Playboy*, with artfully draped sheets and lots of shadows, but it was still a bold move for me. Even more important than the photos was the attention that I lavished on myself to prepare: I splurged on a spray tan (if you can't tone it, tan it); professional hair and makeup; and lingerie from a store that didn't also sell groceries.

I was incredibly lucky to have Wendy Alana—a client and friend—behind the lens. She greeted me with a glass of champagne, a bouquet of birthday flowers, and the perfect playlist to set the mood.

I may never show those pictures to anyone (or I might rent a billboard), and it really doesn't matter. This experience allowed me to celebrate myself because I was worth celebrating, and that acknowledgment was the greatest gift of all.

When your purchase fuels your purpose, marks a milestone, or supports your healing, it's *never* an indulgence—it's an investment.

SEVEN OF COINS

The Seven of Coins is setting goals.

This is a very practical card that asks you to take stock of your progress. For me, it's inviting you to reverse engineer the dreams of your future. You're being called to get clear on your goals, reflect on how to achieve them, then mix in a bit of magic to help them grow. Just as the Six of Cups has you pulling metaphoric weeds under a Full Moon when you Burn Your Sh*t, the Seven of Coins wants you to plant some seeds—and doing this on a New Moon gives it a little extra oomph. This New Moon homework isn't as witchy as setting stuff on fire, but it's equally effective:

Start by focusing on a specific area of your life—wealth, health, love, career—or life in general. Create a three-column chart with the headings Past, Present, and Future. Whether you have one chart or ten, it's important to write it out rather than type it out if possible (to help you tap into your intuition). Take some time to contemplate where you've been, where you are at this moment, and where you want to be in the future. Make your Future column long and detailed, then ask yourself: *How do I reverse engineer this? What changes can I make today to be in that future position tomorrow?*

I always use career as an example to show that it's not just the superficial stuff, like getting on LinkedIn or buying new shoes for an interview. It's deeper, more introspective considerations, such as exploring your limiting beliefs about money or the perceived value you bring to a company. What bad habits do you have that this future, more successful version of you doesn't have? What kind of morning routine sets a framework for success that your future self has?

Take the necessary time to self-reflect in an honest way. Write down action steps and mindset shifts that will help you transition from where you are to where you want to be. Then, get a little witchy with it (because, obviously) by folding that paper up and slipping it under your pillow to sleep on. When you do the laundry, don't burn the paper or throw it out. Instead, keep it in your nightstand or tuck it into a book—keep it close and let it percolate.

I've been telling people about this exercise for over a quarter century because I've seen what happens when you get intentional with your actions by setting goals, doing the necessary inner work, and then bringing in a little magic with some witchy business. This manifesting method was taught to me by my tarot mentor (she called it a spell), and it's so effective that it became the foundation of my monthly New Moon workshop. It's also detailed even further in my first book, *Burn Your Sh*t*. Try it yourself and see what happens (because something will happen).

EIGHT OF COINS

The Eight of Coins knows that you're where you need to be.

This young apprentice is working hard, and although he's starting at the bottom, the coins rising above him indicate he's on a dedicated path to success. The Eight of Coins is reassuring you that you're on the right path, so keep working hard and you'll get there eventually. For me, this card goes even deeper: Take another look at this figure. He's hammering away with an expression that says *I get that I'm on the right path, but why can't I be at the top with everyone else? I'm just as good as those ding-dongs, maybe even better, so why not me?*

The Eight of Coins reminds you that experts don't skip steps; they do the work. You're going in the right direction, and you're exactly where you need to be (even if it's not where you *want* to be). If you tried to cut corners or got plopped on top tomorrow, it would be a hot mess because you need to meet the person, acquire the skill, or learn the lesson that ensures success when you *do* get there. And you will get there—when it's your time.

Unfortunately, you don't get to decide when that happens because our timing is rarely in sync with Divine timing, especially when we want something so badly that a year feels like a century. But for the Divine, a century is just a drop in the bucket. And that bucket? It's an ocean.

Keep your eye on the prize as you move in the direction of your goals. You'll get there when you get there, and at some point, you'll have the perspective to look back and see why it happened that way. We always want to know in advance rather than in retrospect, but that's not how it works.

This card also warns against comparing yourself to others along the way. Remember, where focus goes, energy flows. If you're too busy watching what everyone else is doing (*Look at her! And him!*), you'll end up like the tube dude in front of the hot tub store—flopping everywhere but getting nowhere. Focus on your own ambitions instead of getting distracted by the shiny stuff and what everyone else is doing—mind your business.

The journey is the destination, and paths are created by walking, not waiting. There is no gold at the end of the rainbow because the rainbow *is* the gold.

NINE OF COINS

The Nine of Coins brings the power of finances and the Divine Feminine.

This independent woman is affluent enough to afford the luxuries in life ("We're getting the five-ply toilet paper because we're super fancy now . . ."), but the Nine of Coins is so much more than financial prosperity.

This is a solitary lady wearing beautiful robes, surrounded by her money, land, home, and falcon—all things that women historically couldn't acquire on their own. She is alone but never lonely. She is strong, self-sufficient, and whole. If she's with someone, it's because she *wants* to be, not because she *needs* to be. She doesn't need anyone to tell her she's great—she already knows it. Her validation and fulfillment are an inside job.

She has stepped fully into the strength of her Divine Feminine—now it's your turn.

The Divine Feminine is an energy that resides in all living things. She is empowered from within and boldly speaks her truth, embraces her sexuality, and shows up in her life fully and authentically. She holds the secret to your soul's purpose. Divine Feminine energy is creation and inspiration, peace and harmony, honor and respect. It can be found underneath all of the programming and beliefs that we've inherited or absorbed. When the Nine of Coins appears, she's recognizing the effort you've made to step into this sacred energy while encouraging you to embody it even more.

Give your inner Goddess a voice—she has a lot to say.

TEN OF COINS

The Ten of Coins is the most reassuring card in the deck.

This elderly man is at home with his money, land, pets, and family. Whether they're his material possessions like heirlooms or his memories and traditions, he is surrounded by the fruits of his labor, which he has cultivated over a lifetime to form his legacy.

The Ten of Coins tells you that one day you'll be the old guy. Your future is on the horizon waiting for you; you haven't veered off course. There will be twists and turns, and peaks and valleys along the way, but you're getting there.

So take this card, along with any worries associated with it, and tuck it away for a couple of decades. You've got plenty going on right now—don't add unnecessary stress by worrying about what the last day on earth looks like. There's a lot of life to live before then.

People ultimately want a tarot reading to tell them *It's gonna be okay*, and I always tell my clients that's not how it works. (Tarot is more like *Homework, homework, homework...*)

This is the closest a card gets to telling you: *It's gonna be okay.*

PAGE OF COINS

The Page of Coins urges you to be your own sugar daddy.

This kid's got big plans for making it big. He's holding up his coin to admire it while dreaming of ways to get more. When it comes to money-making ideas or opportunities, the Page of Coins says "Go for it."

Your plan is worth pursuing, so don't shove it in a drawer and forget about it. But it also needs to be strategically cultivated, with careful planning and due diligence. This new idea requires nurturing, like a tender little seedling, until the roots are strong enough to really stick.

You can be aspiring to entrepreneurial greatness or strategizing a raise at your current job, thinking of selling your home or applying for a loan, preparing a settlement or paying off a debt—any money goals that haven't been put into action need to be explored.

The quantity of cash might be modest, but the quality is outstanding. Make the case for your overdue promotion. Switch up the studio apartment for a two-bedroom unit. Ditch the daydreaming when it comes to launching your side hustle, and take action, understanding that you'll also need to be patient before the bucks start rolling in.

The money mojo is there, waiting to be worked on.

KNIGHT OF COINS

The Knight of Coins offers cash or closure (or both).

Some cards have multiple meanings depending on what's being asked, their position in the spread, or the cards around them. The Knight of Coins is a great example; you can look at it in a couple of ways, and (spoiler alert) both are positive.

This card can indicate tying up loose ends to provide some much-needed resolution for a situation that's been dragging on for far too long. Whether you perceive this as positive or negative in the moment, it's ultimately great because it closes one chapter to make space for what comes next.

The Knight of Coins can also indicate reliable money coming in after dogged determination and hard work. Not winning-the-lottery cash, but definitely something comfortable, such as a modest raise, pension kicking in, or settlement being signed. It's steady money that follows consistent effort.

Whether it's seeing a situation through to the end or getting a solid financial infusion—or a combination of the two—the Knight of Coins is a card that I'm always happy to see.

QUEEN OF COINS

The Queen of Coins is wisdom earned and lessons learned.

Meet the most highly evolved Queen in the deck. The Queen of Coins knows who she is because she has dealt with her issues and is comfortable in her skin. The criticism, dissatisfaction, and impatience of youth have transformed into forgiveness, acceptance, and celebration.

She is the crone—mature, wise, and confident of her place in the world. You might be way too young to be her yet, but this Queen assures you that you're on the right path. Keep stepping into the Queen of Coins' wise energy and generous spirit—she has transformed her wounds into wisdom and is the perfect role model of a life well lived.

KING OF COINS

The King of Coins is the Boss.

Like his Queen, the King of Coins has sorted out his shit. He's the most evolved, mature, and confident of Kings. He has no money (or mommy) issues and is a calm, assured leader.

He's often older but can also represent a paternal or authority figure. The King of Coins can be a boss, mentor, or healer. He is responsible, stable, and practical, with a focus on prosperity and security. Like the other Kings, the King of Coins represents the embodiment of these energetic traits in human form—he can be a partner, boss, friend, parent, teacher, or you. You may want to draw another card for this King (and the Queen of Coins too) for context or direction on how to access their energy, but even on their own, they act as a reassuring presence telling you that you're on a good path . . . and there is still work to be done.

∞

Coins cards encompass the material world and earthly matters. They provide solid ground to stand on as well as the fertile soil to cultivate our dreams. Their responsible energy can sometimes be sluggish, but these cards bolster our resources, encourage resilience, and promote responsibility.

∞

As you can see, each Minor Arcana suit has a distinct vibe, and our everyday experiences are a blend of these four approaches. Your tarot readings will show you how the different suit energies are impacting your life at any given moment. For example, if you know that aces signify new opportunities and Wands are about passion and purpose, then the Ace of Wands can be a new chapter that feeds your heart and soul.

Although the suits have defining characteristics (Wands are passion, Cups are emotion, Swords are intellect, and Coins are money), a card from a specific suit can pertain to any area of life. The Two of Coins is a great example: He's juggling his coins and trying not to drop them, but the meaning of this card highlights the need to let go of time-wasting tasks that may have nothing to do with finances.

While the Major Arcana is known to tell the tale of our collective evolution into enlightenment, the Minor Arcana helps us navigate the challenges and opportunities of daily life. Together, they offer reassurance, guidance, and validation.

CHAPTER 14

∞

Have a Conversation with Your Soul
(Readings)

Congratulations—you made it through the entire deck! Hopefully, you're feeling more familiar with tarot now—you know your Hermit from your Hierophant and your Cups from your Coins. Now it's time to let the cards talk.

Noted tarot fan Carl Jung said, "Learn your theories as well as you can, but put them aside when you touch the miracle of the living soul." I think that's great advice as we move into readings. We'll look at different spreads in the next chapter, but for now, let's keep it simple. Try to focus on pulling one card per question and no more than three; otherwise, a reading can get too confusing and overwhelming.

PRE-READING PREP (SPACE & CEREMONY)

You can do a tarot reading wherever you and your cards happen to be. Any space becomes sacred when you infuse it with meaning and intention. So many new tarot readers get caught up in thinking they need a specific environment to pull cards; their confidence suffers if conditions aren't optimal, when all that's required is their deck.

I've given readings all over the place—from cars and closets to backyards and banquet halls—and since COVID, all of my one-on-one readings are done with Zoom. Regardless of the space I'm in, the quality of my tarot readings remains the same (I now prefer online readings because people seem more at ease and energetically open when they're in the comfort of their homes).

When it comes to doing rituals on your deck to prepare for a reading, I believe cards are best used to complement a larger ritual, rather than being the focus of it. Having said that, light some incense and surround yourself with crystals before pulling cards if that makes you feel good. And if rituals aren't your thing, that's fine too. The more rules you put in place to give a reading, the more difficult you might be making things for yourself. As detailed in Chapter 3, if you want to give your cards a Moon bath, cleanse them by smudging, cover them in a special cloth, keep them on an altar, or protect them with magical incantations, go for it. But remember that you don't *need* to do any of that. You and your deck are what matter most—everything else is sprinkles on the sundae.

INTENTION IS EVERYTHING

Intention is the pathway to intuition, and every time you work with your cards, you want to be clear on your "why" for doing a reading.

Again, this doesn't have to be an elaborate process. Setting an intention doesn't necessarily mean knowing exactly what you want to accomplish; it creates a space energetically to have a conversation with your deck. On their own, these cards are just pictures printed on paper, but when you put intention behind them and listen to the stories they have to tell, tarot becomes a tool that helps you understand the world and your place in it.

My intention is always the same, and it's also my mission statement: Inspire, empower, and enlighten. You can use this for your readings or create your own. You could also change it for every reading to meet the moment you're in. If you're unsure of an intention, something along the lines of *May I give guidance for the greatest good and highest healing of this person* will do nicely.

NOT THAT KIND OF KNOCK KNOCK

Before every reading, even just pulling a single card for someone at an event, I knock on the top of my deck a few times. I learned about this energetic palate cleanser from my tarot mentor, Erica, as a way to disperse the previous reading. At this point, it's an instinct that prepares me and my cards to do a reading; I don't even realize I'm doing it.

The people you read are sometimes referred to as the seeker or querent (I call them client), and you'll need to decide if you want them handling your cards, which is a matter of personal preference. Some tarot readers keep a separate deck to work with themselves and have another for public readings. My cards have been used for every reading I've ever done; although, I recently stopped letting people shuffle my deck because they were too rough. Before that, I would always tell clients, "No fancy Vegas moves because I like the cards facing the same direction," but it was also to prevent creasing or ripping them. The majority of my readings are on Zoom, so it's not even an issue, but for in-person events, I tell people my cards are like senior citizens, so I do all the shuffling, but they still get to cut the deck and pick the cards (people *love* to touch tarot cards).

I always prepare people for the "awkward stare" while I shuffle (it's really just me looking at them very intently). This deliberate act of mixing up the cards might take you a couple of seconds or a few minutes, and you can shuffle a specific number of times or stop when it feels right; there is no hard-and-fast rule. Tarot cards are typically bigger than playing cards, and doing a standard shuffle may prove difficult for you, especially if you're brand new to tarot. If this is the case, try the hand-over-hand method, or just put them in a bunch of piles and pick them back up in a different order. Whether done by you or the person you're reading, shuffling is another way to clear your deck while also tapping into the energy of a person, or yourself.

Once the deck has been shuffled, place it face down on a flat surface and cut it using the nondominant hand. You can cut the deck into two piles or twenty; just make sure you use the opposite hand from the one you write with because it acts as a shortcut to your intuition.

After you've asked your question (we'll get to that in a minute), choose a card in a way that resonates for you. You could fan them out and close your eyes before pulling one, or try cutting the deck in half or pulling a card from the top. You may want to make a big, messy pile and grab whichever one jumps out at you.

Speaking of jumping out . . . my agent, Alex (*I love you, Alex!*), relies on cards popping out while she's shuffling, essentially letting the cards choose themselves. When cards go flying in my readings, it's usually a sign that I'm tired, but I do note them, and if they show up again I know it's a message with an exclamation point. Although I don't personally follow Alex's jumper method, I love it because it shows how flexible tarot can be, with nothing set in stone. If you pull cards with intention, try paying attention to (or at least get curious about) any cards that leap out at you—or work with both! This is your practice: Do what works for you.

However a card is pulled, I always have a peek before showing my client because some cards, like Death or The Devil, are alarming at first glance and need a disclaimer so the person doesn't jump to conclusions (or out of their skin).

For example, I preface the Death card by saying, "You got one of my top three cards—I love getting it—and it's also the card that makes people pee themselves a bit because it looks so scary, but I promise it's not . . ." Once they see the card, I reassure them that it never means physical death of a plant, pet, or person; the scary part is connected to their relationship with change (then I go into the full interpretation that was in Chapter 9).

My work is generally done online, so I always see the cards first, but if I'm doing an in-person reading with a spread (more on spreads in Chapter 16) and a worrisome-looking card appears, I'll address it in the moment so they aren't distracted or freaked out. For example, "We'll get to The Devil shortly, but it's nothing satanic or scary. He's just an asshole."

ARE YOU THERE, TAROT? IT'S ME, MARGARET . . . (HOW TO ASK QUESTIONS)

A client recently told me she googled *How to ask the right question in a tarot reading* to prepare for our call. She's not the first person to do this.

Asking the right types of questions can make or break a tarot reading. So what goes into a good question? The best ones elicit information that empowers you to make optimal decisions for yourself or a situation. They focus on what you can influence or change in a positive and constructive way, what to avoid or watch out for, or how to look at things from a different perspective.

Good questions are open-ended because there aren't generally *yes* or *no* cards (although some are more positive or negative in tone), and you need to provide space to explore different options or possibilities in a way that still allows for focus and direction.

The following questions are helpful starting points:

What stands in the way of my goal, and how can I best overcome it?
How can I improve my ability to . . . ?
What role do I play in so-and-so's life/issue?
What do I need to change in order to . . . ?
What is the potential for . . . ?
How can I have more fun in life?
How can I invite more peace into my life?
What do I need to cultivate more of in my life?
How can I tap into my creativity?
What do I need to release?
How can I attain freedom?
What am I currently neglecting?
What is my biggest challenge at the moment?
What area of my life needs the most attention right now?
How can I feel more connected in my relationships?
What do I need to focus on right now?

One of the easiest (and most effective) ways to phrase a question in an open-ended way is with the phrase *What do I need to know about . . . ?* because the cards will always have something to say.

If the initial question is, "Should I quit my job?" try asking, "What do I need to know about looking for a new job?" Instead of asking, "Is Fred the one?" try rephrasing it as, "What do I need to know about my relationship with Fred?"

Make sure you're focusing on yourself (or the person you're

reading) rather than other people when you ask a question because tarot isn't about dipping into their energy as much as gaining insight around how to deal with them. Keeping the spotlight on you emphasizes responsibility and accountability, reinforcing your free will.

Instead of asking, "Does Sergio regret leaving me for Daphne?" restate it as, "What do I need to know about my relationship with Sergio?" or even better, "What do I need to know about future romance?" See the difference? Even if you ask the first version, the answer will almost certainly focus on you instead of bothering with Sergio's thoughts on the matter. We don't give a crap about Sergio because it's not his reading—this is about what's best for *you*.

Sometimes the cards will have their own ideas about things. I tell my clients that tarot always provides an answer—it just might not be what they want to hear. A message could have nothing to do with the question being asked but still resonate with the person asking. Or the question might have been too specific ("Will I go to Harvard or Princeton?"). Maybe it was asked in a yes/no format. In any case, it's like the cards are saying, *"Your question was cute, but here's what you really need to know right now.* As well, if you've been asking the same thing over and over in the hopes of getting a different response, the cards might be telling you it's time to move on and talk about something else.

Take a moment to consider the insight being offered and trust what shows up—because it's showing up for a reason.

NUH-UH (WHAT NOT TO ASK)

In the same way that framing a question properly is essential for an insightful and powerful tarot reading, knowing what *not* to ask is also crucial.

I always steer clear of asking for specific names, diagnoses, and deadlines because tarot cards can't give you the name of your soulmate, the cause of your stomachache, or the day you'll start your dream job.

Faulty timelines can lead to self-fulfilling prophecies. For instance, if I tell Barb that she'll be in love by the first of July, she might find herself desperately scrolling through Tinder on the last day of June, ready to settle for the next match just because the tarot reader said so (or she might go for the first guy who comes along, hoping to make the prediction come true). Offering any form of guarantee will likely warp poor Barb's perceptions and decisions around dating. It's also generally best not to set a time frame that is beyond a year; so much can change (or stay the same) in that time because you have free will. I clearly state at the beginning of my readings that the messages cover from now until six-to-nine months out. The cards merely reflect the energy of your current landscape along with what's possible in the immediate future. Any time frame that's too long veers into fortune-telling territory (and that's woo woo *with* the cuckoo).

Below are some examples of questions to avoid, why we avoid them (as we saw in Chapter 7), and potential reframes where possible.

Will my lover leave his wife? Will my partner ever change?
Asking questions about areas of another person's life that have nothing to do with you violates their privacy. You're essentially using the cards to trespass into someone else's energy. Focus on what you need to know about dealing with your relationship (or better yet, how you can move on from a dysfunctional dynamic).

Why does my sister hate me?
Questions steeped in negative emotions aren't helpful because the nature of these questions is extremely disempowering, and you can't change someone else's opinion. Instead, ask "What can I do

to improve my relationship with my sister?" or "What do I need to know about my relationship with my sister?" If you want to drill a little deeper into your own development and growth, you might ask "What do I need to improve within myself to create better relationships with others?"

What is the name of my soulmate?
Again, tarot doesn't do names and you don't want to limit yourself to people with *W* names because a so-called psychic foretold it. A better use of your time and the cards' energy is to focus on what you need to know about future romance or how you can evolve as a person so you're able to invite the ideal love into your life (making romance a beautiful by-product rather than the goal).

Should I take that job?
Any *Should I . . . ?* questions are difficult for the cards to address because they're asking for yes/no answers and they're also very disempowering (if you read about Judgement in Chapter 9, you've hopefully banished "shoulds" from your vocabulary). Tarot wants you to take responsibility for your life and your choices. When you ask *Should I . . . ?* questions, you're surrendering accountability. Try asking "What do I need to know about that job offer?" because it lets the cards shine a light on the energetic landscape—showing you what's happening, what's possible, and what to be aware of—and allows you to make the best decision for yourself.

Will my mother's health improve?
Never use tarot (or Google) as a substitute for medical advice. Ask how you can best support your mother and be prepared for the answer to focus less on the other person and more on what you can do for yourself to best deal with your mother's situation.

Thinking that you must consult your deck before making any decision will ultimately undermine your personal growth. Watch that you don't become dependent on the cards: They're meant to support you in taking responsibility for your choices and actions, not take over. When used correctly, tarot is a tool that helps you discover the wisdom within.

IT'S TAROT'S TURN TO TALK
(LISTENING TO YOUR CARDS)

Now that you've mastered the best way to ask a question, how do you interpret the card you've pulled for the answer?

Take a moment to reflect on the imagery of your card and how it makes you feel. What words, images, or phrases come to mind? Are you having any physical sensations, like a tingle in your tummy, head-to-toe goose bumps, or instant IBS symptoms? Does it offer clear guidance or bring up more questions? Note your reaction—not in relation to the conventional tarot definitions, but in what it means to you. Absorb the story of the card and apply it to your question, situation, or life in general. Grab your tarot journal and record your initial thoughts before looking at external meanings, and don't be discouraged if you find that your reaction to a card is at odds with the traditional (or Tarot Lori) interpretation—noticing these differences is how you deepen the relationship with your deck. As you gain experience with the cards, you'll learn to trust the meanings that work for you and leave the rest.

My approach to tarot often drills beneath the traditional meaning to look at the root cause of why or how a story is showing up as well as how to address it. For example, the Five of Coins is typically about poverty, but my interpretation advises you to be more detail-oriented so things don't slip through the cracks (which could then lead to poverty or other unfortunate outcomes).

Your first impressions of a card can be packed with intuitive insight. Pay attention to what comes to mind in the moment. When you get an image or a word or a feeling or a sensation, that's where the message—and the magic—can be found.

I DON'T GET IT
(WHAT TO DO WHEN CARDS MAKE NO SENSE)

Sometimes the cards you pull have no apparent correlation to your question, especially when it comes to the Minor Arcana (e.g., you get a bunch of Cups when asking about work, or Coins when questioning romance). You can always pull a clarifying card if the first one has you stumped, but don't be too quick to dismiss your initial message—adding another layer could make things even more confusing.

In my readings, crossovers happen all the time. For example, the message of the Three of Wands (get off your ass and start moving toward your goals) can apply to any area of life. Same goes for the unclenching directive from the Five of Swords.

Maybe the card you initially drew encouraged you to get curious; by offering a different perspective (rather than a clear answer), the cards are inviting you to consider other possibilities and solve your own problems, which will inevitably boost your confidence and bolster self-belief in your abilities.

To help you connect to the card, speak its name out loud as you look at it, then close your eyes and take a few deep, grounding breaths. Notice anything that comes up during this meditative moment, and when you're ready, open your eyes and look at it again. Consider any symbols or color combinations that jump out. Do they connect to you in a special way? Maybe a featured animal is personally significant to you. What does the action (or stillness) in the image mean to you? Does a figure's facial expression convey a specific story? How does any of this pertain to your current situation?

Try visualizing yourself within the card's story, and let your imagination run wild. Maybe have a conversation with the people in the image; ask them what's going on and see how they respond. Most importantly, trust your intuition.

If a card still makes no sense in relation to the question asked (or it's a snooze like The Hierophant and doesn't give much information on its own), you can always pull another card for context. If the next one has a similar theme, consider that it's your deck's way of saying *Weren't you paying attention the first time?*

As you get more comfortable with tarot, look for ways to connect the messages to modern life. Use relatable examples to demonstrate meanings, especially when reading for others. This helps you weave the narrative of the cards into a beautiful tapestry of insight.

Here's an example of how to do this with The Tower, which is about removing our blinders by teaching us big lessons. These lessons can seem scary, and they're definitely difficult, but they're not always negative. To illustrate this point, I always share a story from my life as a newlywed, when my husband and I were too busy blowing our money on stupid stuff to focus on our future—until I unexpectedly got pregnant (#notthatkindofpsychic). Although my son was an absolute blessing—and he's just graduated college, so I'd say things turned out well—it was still an incredibly challenging time that was also completely necessary.

The Four of Cups and Eight of Coins offer another example. Both feature the same figure in different situations, and in each instance, his expression is kind of *meh*. The first card is a case of too much daydreaming leading to Divine discontent, while the second warns of avoiding shortcuts to get ahead. His dissatisfied vibe in both helped me cultivate each story, shaping my interpretations in a way that makes them relatable in my readings.

SKEPTICS & SCAREDY-CATS
(READING FOR THE RELUCTANT)

Obviously (I hope), you never force a reading on anyone—this isn't like *Long Island Medium* where you ambush some unsuspecting soul at the deli counter and demand to deliver a message—but if you pull cards for someone who was pressured to get a reading by a spouse or friend, chances are good that reading will be bad. These days I quite enjoy the challenge of having a person (usually a man) sit in front of me at an event, his arms crossed in defiance, daring me to make him a believer. A few minutes later, I usually have to shoo him away because he's hooked and won't stop asking questions.

When a person is closed off—out of fear, mistrust, or skepticism—it's like an energetic drawbridge is raised, and I feel like I'm talking to a wall. In these moments, I just carry on because I know that it's not my job to convince anyone that tarot works or if I'm any good at it—my role is to deliver the messages tarot has to tell. Eventually, I'll mention something or they'll ask a question, and the energy comes rushing through in a giant whoosh as resistance evaporates. My goose bumps (aka goosies) go next level, and everything starts to flow much easier.

Sometimes clients will get defensive during a reading (*This doesn't sound like me at all!*) because they don't like what they're hearing. Or they're genuinely confused by a card's message and how it applies to them. When I was starting out, this feedback would send me spiraling into a panic, feeling like a failure and a fraud. Looking back, I can see how my reaction reflected my own confusion and insecurity about the cards and their meanings. As my interpretations evolved, my connection to the cards deepened, and my confidence as a tarot reader grew. Now I have no problem pushing back on people who resist what the cards are conveying, explaining that these cards turned up for a reason and may pertain to something down the road (because my readings relate from now until six-to-nine months out) or might be something that's meant to be contemplated for a bit. It's not always what they're expecting, but it's what tarot wants them to know.

This is one reason I record my readings. I talk for an hour, and it's a lot to take in, so I encourage people to listen to the recording after a bit of time has passed and they've processed the information. I get a lot of feedback from clients telling me how something that didn't register at all during their reading makes total sense when they listen again. And I always provide an opportunity for clients to ask as many questions as they want, but I leave questions until the end because whatever they've come to me for is usually addressed in the main part of the reading. In addition to pulling cards for guidance around their question, I'll always refer back to the main spread because the answer is in there and just needs to be explained in the context of their question.

Also, whenever I read someone familiar with tarot, I make sure to mention that my interpretations may differ from what they're used to, but in the context of our reading, my meanings are the ones we'll be using. You may want to do the same.

REVERSALS

A reversed tarot card is what it sounds like: a card that's pulled with the image upside down. Some people just turn it right side up and keep going, while others view it as significant with alternate interpretations. Reversals are often misunderstood to be negative, but they're generally thought to be pointing out potential blocks of a card's energy or identifying underlying issues. You could choose to see a reversal as an amplification of that card's original message, or you could correlate upright cards with the outer world and reversals with the inner. You may find that reversals give your readings an added layer of depth or decide they're completely unnecessary (as a newbie, they might be more overwhelming than enlightening). Try both interpretations, and feel free to switch back and forth as you get comfortable with your deck. As the relationship with your cards strengthens, they'll respond to whichever strategy you choose.

It's a matter of personal preference; your readings won't be better or worse just because a card is upside down. Use your intuition to determine what enhances your experience. And remember, just like with cards that are upright, there is no "right" way to learn the meaning of reversals, and your interpretations may evolve over time.

To figure out what reversals mean for you, pick a card and turn it upside down to look at it. See it as if for the first time, and ask yourself how it makes you feel to view it inverted. You may notice aspects about the reversed card that weren't apparent when it was upright. Do the symbols, colors, or characters have a different significance? Is the meaning altered or emphasized? Are you simply annoyed that they aren't all facing the same direction? If you decide to use reversals, be flexible regarding their purpose. For example, Death reversed might indicate barriers to transformation while a reversed Tower might mean it's time for rebuilding.

Reversals have never been my thing. I was taught by Erica to always keep my cards upright because it keeps the energy flowing smoothly in the same direction (some people do this with their money). I also find that my interpretations already provide plenty of information and touch on a lot of themes without relying on reversals—if I added another layer of complexity, my readings would be five hours long.

SHOW & TELL (SAMPLE READINGS)

In my tarot workshops I always pull cards to demonstrate how their meanings can be applied to specific questions, and I thought it would be helpful for you as well. Here are some examples of common questions I have asked the cards about friends (with their permission, of course) and how I interpreted the answers:

QUESTION: What do I need to know about my marriage?
CARD: Eight of Cups
INTERPRETATION: On the surface, this card looks bleak because the figure is disillusioned and turning his back on whatever (or whomever) is no longer in alignment. This card asks you to leave behind what isn't working so you can get to the good stuff that's waiting around the corner. The Moon signifies all of the stress and fear around the unknown, but joy and abundance are waiting on the other side; he's just not there yet. This might mean leaving a relationship, but it could also be a toxic friend-

ship that interferes with your married dynamic. It might refer to how you're communicating or the way you deal with money. Maybe it's looking for a new home or different kind of diet. Get curious about what isn't working, and don't be afraid to seek out alternatives, knowing that, in doing so, you're creating capacity for something better.

QUESTION: What do I need to know about going back to school?
CARD: Three of Wands
INTERPRETATION: This card is a kick in the butt, telling you that when it comes to the goals or intentions you've set (in this case, school), it's time to get moving. Plan the work so you can work the plan. Don't wait for optimal conditions or perfect timing because they will never happen and you'll stay stuck on the sidelines of your life. You'll be able to change your direction once you go, but you need to go. Forget about the finish line—focus on next steps.

QUESTION: What do I need to know about looking for a new job?
CARD: Five of Swords
INTERPRETATION: It's time to unclench and stop trying to control outcomes because these behaviors are keeping you from moving forward energetically (also, it's not control; it's anxiety). Are you clenched about a new job having to meet your specific requirements, such as a certain company or location, or exact timelines? Are you focused on what's horrible in your current job or fixated on an opportunity you didn't get? Think of your job search like baking a cake: You can have all of the ingredients, follow exact instructions, and put it in the oven at the right temperature, but after that, it's out of your hands. There's nothing else to do except surrender to the process, knowing that whatever happens, happens. You've done your part and that's enough. Exhale.

QUESTION: What do I need to know about my passion project?
CARD: Two of Swords
INTERPRETATION: The fear and doubt you're feeling is unfounded. The figure's blindfold signifies not even knowing why you're feeling this way or what exactly is keeping you stuck—and maybe you're not meant to know—but the water behind her is calm, indicating that there's nothing to warrant all of the worry. You can either put yourself out there in ways that might feel scary, vulnerable, and untested (such as starting an Instagram account or applying to sell your products at a local market) and realize it's not as scary as you anticipated . . . or you can stay stuck. The choice is yours.

QUESTION: What do I need to know about my spiritual evolution?

CARD: Three of Coins

INTERPRETATION: This is traditionally a money card, but in my readings it can apply to any area of life, and the message remains the same: It's time to step things up a notch. You have a solid base that you can now build upon, whether that's taking a course, going on a retreat, meditating a little longer, or deepening your relationship with Spirit in a way that resonates with you. You're ready to level up, and your foundation is stronger than you may think.

QUESTION: What do I need to know about my dad's health? (Note: I reframed this to "How can I support my dad regarding his health?")

CARD: Two of Coins

INTERPRETATION: This card reflects extremely busy energy. You're spinning plates on sticks, trying to keep them all from crashing, and you need to figure out which plates truly require your attention and which ones you can delegate or drop. This might be within your home (e.g., asking your partner to make dinner more often) or determining which timelines are most flexible at work. It could mean arranging outside care or help from another family member to assist with your dad's well-being. Or speaking with his healthcare team about optimizing his treatment plan. Looking at areas with energy leaks will benefit everyone, including your dad. Also consider which pressures might be self-imposed out of a sense of obligation to prove yourself in some way—that's not necessary, and it's unhelpful to everyone, especially you.

∞

Do you see how much insight you can get from a single card? And how a card can support you spiritually, guide next steps, affirm your decision, offer consolation, or kick your ass? Isn't tarot *amazing*?!?

THE SECRET SAUCE
(HOW TO MAKE A GOOD READING GREAT)

If you're like me, you'll open your deck and immediately want to start pulling cards for friends and family—and you definitely need to practice on them—but please watch that you aren't relying on other people for confirmation that you're "doing it right."

Seeking outside validation instead of believing in yourself doesn't serve anyone (in tarot or life). The spotlight needs to be on the person getting the reading rather than how you're doing as a reader. The cards can have an energy to them that is fun, sexy, difficult, combative, easy, or inspiring ... and again, what the seeker does with the information offered is completely up to them. As tarot readers, we are simply the messenger, or interpreter.

It used to be awkward when I first started reading strangers because some didn't want to tell me anything in advance—which is fine, and I've always preferred reading people cold over reading family members or close friends because I can be more objective—but in the beginning, it felt like I was being tested, so there was an element of guesswork, which can jack up your stress and shut off intuition. Now I always ask clients if they're married or in a romantic situation. I ask everyone this question in order to cut to the chase, and I joke that I'm not that kind of psychic, which sets expectations while putting people at ease. Clearly state at the beginning that what you're doing is not fortune-telling. You don't have to "prove" yourself by telling people where Grandma hid the good jewelry before she died.

My goal with tarot is to inspire, empower, and enlighten people so they can heal, guide, and love themselves—which is impossible if I'm worried about their opinion of me. It took me years to realize that looking for confirmation from the person I was reading made the experience all about me. Flipping the focus changed everything.

When it comes to reading tarot cards, the difference between doubt and trust is confidence—and that comes with practice and patience.

∞

Tarot reflects the human condition: the good, the bad, and the ugly. The cards will never leave you hanging or feeling worse—they always offer a perspective to consider, a nudge to be acknowledged, solace in being seen, or homework to be done that helps you get through the rough stuff and step into your greatness.

As you develop a dialogue with your deck, the vocabulary may shift over time. You may even put your deck aside and stop speaking for a bit. But if you remain open and curious to what the cards have to say, you're in for a juicy conversation that will be eternal.

CHAPTER 15

∞

Sticks & Stars
(Tarot & Astrology)

Throughout the Middle Ages, astrology and astronomy were seen as sister sciences. Many distinguished academic institutions had astrology chairs, including Cambridge University, and astrologers were commonly found in royal courts. The Enlightenment led to a spiritual purgatory as reason and science were valued over superstition and blind faith, and the distinction between astrology and astronomy widened. But astrology never went away—from royalty to world leaders, people of influence still seek counsel from the sky.

I'm not an astrologer, but I love astrology (if you're looking for an expert, Heidi Rose Robbins and Chani Nicholas are two of my faves). The tarot spread that I use in my readings was created by my mentor, Erica, and although it has evolved over three decades into my own thing, it has an astrological foundation (I go into detail in Chapter 16). For fans of the zodiac, assigning a sign to every tarot card is a great way to familiarize yourself with your deck and even longtime tarot readers can look to the stars to deepen their connection with the cards.

ASTROLOGY 101

The zodiac signs of an astrological chart (or wheel) are divided by degrees, and each of the twelve signs contains thirty degrees. Although the French occultist Etteilla was the first, in the 1700s, to design a tarot deck with astrological attributes, the connection between the stars and cards was reinforced indelibly by the creators of the *Rider-Waite-Smith* tarot deck in 1909. Both A. E. Waite and Pamela Colman Smith were members of the Hermetic Order of the Golden Dawn, a metaphysical collective that developed an elaborate system to categorize every tarot card with a corresponding element, planet, or sign. (It looks like an astrology wheel on steroids.)

This classification lines up the sequence of the cards with the structure of the zodiac, but I don't put much stock in their configuration. For one thing, they conveniently ditched the Page cards to make everything fit, so it doesn't reflect the deck in its entirety. I don't believe that this arrangement considers the individual essence of each card or the characteristics of every sign. It seems somewhat random and leaves very little room for personal interpretation.

The point of tarot and astrology is to help you make sense of the world and your place in it. You see your relationship to the cards through the lens of your life, and if that differs from the conventions of the last century, that's okay. Your interpretation of a card's astrological sign is just as personal to you as the meaning of the card itself. Using the Strength card as an example, when determining which astrological sign is the strongest, you have to consider what strength means to you. Is it physical fortitude? Intellectual might? Emotional resilience? Creative power? Never feel obligated to follow a certain system, but do feel free to experiment with astrology, numerology, or any other tradition that tickles your esoteric fancy.

What follows are the key traits of each zodiac sign, along with their traditional tarot counterpart and my interpretation (spoiler: Mine are all different). This illustrates how you can intuit the connections in ways that support your tarot practice. And if you disagree with my hot tarot takes, that's okay too! Tarot works best when you figure out what works for you.

ARIES

KEY TRAITS: The ram is known for being brave and bold, being confident in what it wants, and fearlessly going after it. The energy of Aries is direct, impulsive, and assured in its goals. An Aries would make a great rodeo clown, contestant on *Survivor*, or professional adrenaline junkie.
TRADITIONAL TAROT: The Emperor is steeped in structure, discipline, stability, and security.
MY INTERPRETATION: The Fool is the first card of the Major Arcana (just as Aries is the first sign of the zodiac). But more importantly, both share an impulsive quality that is prone to acting before thinking, courageously leaping into life.

TAURUS

KEY TRAITS: The grounded bull loves to indulge in earthly pleasures, luxuriating in life's finer things. Taurus is the quintessential homebody, resistant to change and slow to get moving, but very steadfast and determined to keep going when the going gets tough. A Taurus would be tickled to work as a food blogger, athleisure wear tester, or literal hermit (who wears Hermès).

TRADITIONAL TAROT: The Hierophant, often referred to as the Pope or spiritual guide of tarot, is rooted in tradition, teaching, and obedience.

MY INTERPRETATION: The Empress is a juicy card of fertile femininity. Her lush energy aligns with Venus, the planet that rules Taurus and is associated with love, beauty, and pleasure.

GEMINI

KEY TRAITS: Gemini is the chattiest sign in the sky, with a keen intellect that can adapt to any situation. This extroverted energy has an insatiable curiosity that's eager to synthesize and share every morsel of information it encounters with the world at large. Geminis make great politicians, talk show hosts, and TikTokkers.

TRADITIONAL TAROT: The Lovers, which depicts two halves of a whole, combine their energy in a perfect union (this is a bit too on the nose for me).

MY INTERPRETATION: The Eight of Wands has a turbo-charged energy associated with kick-starting momentum, clear communication, and swift progress.

CANCER

KEY TRAITS: Sensitivity, thy name is Cancer. The crab brings its home everywhere because home is everything. This is a nurturing, compassionate, and highly emotional sign prone to codependency if left unchecked. Ideal career choices include nursery-school teacher, greeting-card writer, and professional hugger.

TRADITIONAL TAROT: The Chariot is all about overcoming obstacles to achieve success through sheer grit, determination, and willpower.

MY INTERPRETATION: The Moon is a clear choice for me because it's the luminary that rules Cancer, but also because it invites the fortification of boundaries in all forms to protect your energy.

LEO

KEY TRAITS: This magnetic lion never met a spotlight it didn't want to step into. Leo energy is supremely confident, fiercely ambitious, and ferociously loyal—boisterous, exuberant, and bursting with creativity. A Leo would thrive as an Academy Award winner, prima ballerina, or CEO of anything.
TRADITIONAL TAROT: Strength is a powerful card focusing on persistence, stamina, courage, and patience. (It also features a big lion, which seems a bit obvious.)
MY INTERPRETATION: The Sun exudes positive, confident, and radiant energy that indicates an abundance of success, vitality, and luck (bonus: The Sun also rules Leo).

VIRGO

KEY TRAITS: Virgos love a to-do list like chips love salsa. Detail-oriented and deeply analytical, Virgo energy seeks to be of service. Having such high standards can come across as judgemental perfectionism, but it stems from a place of love and good intentions. Their practical and conscientious nature makes them the perfect editor, HGTV host, or spelling bee adjudicator.
TRADITIONAL TAROT: The Hermit asks you to take time for introspection so you can seek solutions from within.
MY INTERPRETATION: Justice is related to karmic ebb and flow in my readings, and Virgo—one of the most dedicated and diligent signs of the zodiac—exemplifies the idea that you get what you give, and results come from consistent effort.

LIBRA

KEY TRAITS: Libra energy is rooted in relationships, balance, and beauty. Their inherent empathy and charm make flirting an extreme sport, while solitude and conflict are their kryptonite. A Libra would excel at being a professional matchmaker, diplomat, or cult member.

TRADITIONAL TAROT: Justice is the obvious choice because of the balance (with literal scales), fairness, and compromise.

MY INTERPRETATION: The Ten of Cups represents happiness, harmony, and family. For me, it's a card of connections, emphasizing the need to lean on and leverage all relationships because family comes in many forms.

SCORPIO

KEY TRAITS: Scorpio energy is intense and complex, diving deep into the shadows to reveal hidden truths. They neither forgive nor forget, and they believe small talk is for suckers. A Scorpio's ability to see beyond the surface makes them great professional poker players, Harlequin antiheroes, or cult leaders.

TRADITIONAL TAROT: Death is a powerful card of transformational change, and I can actually get behind this card for Scorpio, but I also think there's a better one . . .

MY INTERPRETATION: The Devil traditionally reveals lust, greed, envy, and other deadly sins. For me, this card is an invitation to explore, identify, and ultimately heal the wounds that can manifest as addiction, abuse, and servitude. The Devil offers an opportunity to slay the shadows that obstruct transformation.

SAGITTARIUS

KEY TRAITS: Sagittarius is the explorer of the zodiac, on an endless quest for growth and expansion. Their optimism is as infectious as their impulsivity is infuriating. Routine is their enemy, and bad decisions are par for the course. A freedom-seeking Sag would love to be a travel writer, tarot card reader, or real-life Indiana Jones.

TRADITIONAL TAROT: Temperance typically relates to calm, moderation, and equilibrium (which is way off base according to this Sagittarius-rising author).

MY INTERPRETATION: The Knight of Wands is an enthusiastic call to adventure, fizzing with feisty and inspired energy, encouraging life to be lived from a place of YES.

CAPRICORN

KEY TRAITS: Capricorn is the overachieving workhorse of the zodiac, with a strong moral compass and even stronger work ethic. The goat's energy is ambitious, dutiful, and responsible, making them an ideal jury foreman, older sibling, or designated driver.

TRADITIONAL TAROT: The Devil, as noted above, represents being enslaved to dangerous desires and tempting taboos (Capricorns would NEVER).

MY INTERPRETATION: The Emperor symbolizes reason, duty, and patriarchal energy (in my readings, this card can represent a man or The Man). The Emperor's essence aligns with Saturn, the ruling planet of Capricorn—both are focused on discipline, authority, and structure.

AQUARIUS

KEY TRAITS: Aquarius is the quirkiest sign in the sky. Eccentric and unconventional to the core, Aquarius energy prefers to work alone in service of the greater good. Life is perceived as a giant experiment, and weirdness is worn as a badge of honor. An Aquarian would be a great conspiracy theorist, union leader, or mad scientist.

TRADITIONAL TAROT: The Star is a hopeful and inspiring card when confidence has been lost, signifying renewal and faith in the future.

MY INTERPRETATION: The Hermit is an enlightened and innovative thinker who finds wisdom from within.

PISCES

KEY TRAITS: Pisces energy is ephemeral and infinite, imbued with intuition and creativity. Their ethereal nature is overflowing with altruism and empathy, sometimes to a fault. With limitless imagination and a yearning to feel all the things, a Pisces would love to be a professional daydreamer, eighteenth-century poet, or Hobby Lobby manager.

TRADITIONAL TAROT: The Moon symbolizes delusion and deception, focusing on fear and foreboding.

MY INTERPRETATION: The High Priestess is a connection to higher wisdom that can be accessed through intuition, dreams, and other liminal spaces.

∞

Learning more about the relationship between your cards and the stars is a fun way to deepen your understanding of tarot. And you can do it in a way that is intuitive rather than imposed. Remember, astrology isn't a competition (neither is tarot), and every sign has its own strengths and challenges. Just like with the cards, one isn't better or worse than the other—they're just different.

CHAPTER 16

∞

Spread 'Em
(Putting It All Together)

Just one card can give you incredible insight into the day ahead or issue at hand, but if you're ready to expand the story tarot tells, you can pull additional cards and arrange them in a spread.

A tarot spread is the pattern used to display the cards; it provides a framework that allows you to create a cohesive reading. The term "layout" refers to the positioning of the cards within the spread. Each card typically relates to either a specific area of life (love, work, etc.) or some other designation such as "obstacles" or "outcomes," and they fit together like puzzle pieces to give your reading some structure.

You can configure the cards to be as simple or convoluted as you want, but keep in mind that larger spreads can leave you even more confused, while a simple one answers all of your questions with ease.

Even if you're an old-school tarot enthusiast, I would avoid looking at the spreads used by original trailblazers in the early 1900s because your head will explode. Case in point: Samuel L.

MacGregor Mathers, founder of the Hermetic Order of the Golden Dawn (go back to Chapter 1 for more on this esoteric association), offered the following instructions in 1888 for his go-to tarot spread (this is just a snippet from his published pamphlet, but you'll get the idea):

> *Deal the top card on a part of the table which we will call B, the second card on another place which we will call A, into which the whole deck is to be dealt. Then deal the third and fourth cards on B, and the fifth on A; the sixth and seventh on B, and the eighth on A; the ninth and tenth on B, and the eleventh on A. Continue this operation of dealing two cards on B, and one on A, till you come to the end of the pack. Now divide the deck into four stacks with 26, 17, 11, and 24 cards in each respective pile. Put the last pile aside as these cards have no bearing on the question. Arrange the 26 cards face upwards from right to left (being careful not to alter the order), so that they are in the form of a horseshoe, the top card being at the lowest right-hand corner, and the last at the lowest left-hand corner. Read their meanings from right to left so as to make a connected answer, then take the first and last to read their combined meaning, reading the second and second-last cards together and so on until you come to the last pair. Do this with every pile.*

Reading this gave me heartburn (confession: I have a similar reaction to the infamous Celtic Cross). You don't need an elaborate tarot spread to give a great reading. Complex spreads are often confusing and intimidating, and they're completely unnecessary. Selecting just two cards can give you over three thousand combinations.

Trying to wrap your head around seventy-eight different card images is daunting enough, let alone how they interact with each other depending on where they sit in a spread. Get comfortable working with a few cards at a time before branching into intricate configurations. Take a stab at deciphering your spread before turning to any guidebook (including this one). You don't need to memorize every meaning to navigate your reading because the imagery will usually give you a sense of what you're dealing with. If you're using a unique deck with pictures that differ from *Rider-Waite-Smith*, it will reflect the designer's distinct interpretation. But you're also being invited to make those meanings your own, adapting as necessary, and they'll still work—that's the magic of tarot. As you become familiar with the story of each card, you can start combining them to tell a comprehensive tale. Whether that's a brief anecdote or sweeping saga, tarot is simply telling stories.

TOP TIPS

Pay attention to cards that repeat over several readings or keep turning up when you reshuffle because you didn't like that answer the first time: They're hounding you for a reason. Take a moment to meditate on or journal about why a particular card's message is being so persistent (and why you might be resisting it).

Some readers choose to attach the energy of a reading to a specific person or issue by designating one card to be the significator, placing it like a symbol at the top of the spread. For example, The Empress could signify pregnancy, or a King might symbolize you. This significator is assigned before the reading and is meant to provide clarity or depth to the other cards in the spread. I've never understood the point of this extra step because it feels like an attempt to exert control over the reading by putting unnecessary parameters or assumptions in place. If that works for you, go for it. But at the end of the day, the cards know what to do; trust what comes up.

Above all else, don't forget about your intuition. Tarot is a tool to access your inner oracle—honor your instinctive reaction to the cards and how they relate to your question or the person being read.

Ménage à Trois (Three-Card Spreads)

When you're ready to do readings for other people (I mean your sister... don't go charging strangers money for tarot just yet), start with a three-card spread. Ask her to shuffle the deck while she thinks of herself—imagining her name or face in her mind—until she feels they've been shuffled enough. If you're doing the shuffling, stare into her eyes while you do it, and stop when the cards feel ready. Put the deck face down, and have your sister cut the cards with her nondominant hand.

Fan the cards out and have her ask a question out loud to the cards. Make sure it's stated in an open-ended way, such as "What do I need to know about my job/relationship/etc.?" She can also keep it simple and let the cards do their thing by asking, "What do I need to know right now?"

Have her pick three cards (it doesn't matter which hand she uses) and place them face down. She can also take the first three cards from the top of the deck or cut the deck to get three cards—how the cards are chosen is up to you.

Now gather the cards and consider the story of each one before showing your sister. A spread is the sum of its parts, so take time to examine all of the cards. Look for connections or patterns that stand out. It doesn't have to be told in the order they were picked—mix them up to create the message meant to be conveyed. Be open and honest with what you see. You may want to jot down a few notes or refer to your guidebook in the beginning to help you keep track. Notice how they collectively form a larger narrative. You can be expansive and verbose in your explanation or keep things lean with bullet points—communicate it in a way that works for you. If the cards make no sense, tell her the meaning of each card to help determine the message(s) being offered.

Whenever possible, use modern or relevant examples to demonstrate potential meanings—it helps you integrate the story between the cards in meaningful ways. Look for patterns in the cards and combine the messages into a compelling and relatable narrative.

An example is The Hermit: If this card showed up in your reading, I'd tell you that you need to expand your mindfulness practice (or get one) because the answers you're looking for are inside you, accessed by unplugging from the to-do list layer of life and going within. The Hermit wants you in a zone similar to that feeling when you arrive at a destination with no clue how you got there, but with all of your problems solved while you were driving (but don't do it when you're behind the wheel because that's dangerous). Do you see how this one card provides insight in a way that is relatable to most people and includes concrete steps to be taken?

Here is an example of how a three-card spread comes together. I'm pulling these cards right now as I type this (exciting!):

MY QUESTION: What do I need to know about publishing this manuscript?

MY CARDS: Two of Coins, Knight of Wands, and Ace of Cups.

Two of Coins: Very busy energy, like spinning plates. Some of them are delicate while others are cheap plastic, so look at which plates you can drop.
Knight of Wands: Fun! Adventure! Say YES to life! Put out to the Universe that you're ready for excitement, play, action . . . and when opportunities show up, don't miss out because you were too busy doing laundry.

Ace of Cups: Your cup is overflowing with love from all sources, keeping you afloat, and your project comes from the heart.

The Combined Message: Drop the nonessential tasks (I see you, laundry) so you can give your book project the attention it requires because pursuing it is a full-body YES, infused with love, offering fun and exciting adventure—and your loved ones are there to support you along the way.

I have to admit, this is a pretty spot-on message! I'm constantly amazed how the stories of these cards validate where you're at while also tapping into the struggles, challenges, and opportunities for growth that we've been facing for centuries (which is why this century-old deck still resonates today). Although I like to keep things open with three-card spreads and let the message reveal itself, you can also incorporate a variety of different configurations. Here are some of the most common:

Past, Present, Future

This reading looks at the cards side by side, from left to right, in the order that you pull them. It addresses where you've been, where you are, and where you're heading. The order can change depending on your preference (e.g., present, past, future), but regardless of how you place the cards, be sure to assign each card's placement before pulling the card. You can keep it general or apply this formation to a particular area of life, such as romance or finances. Tarot won't make firm predictions, but it can suggest what's possible and give you a sense of the energetic landscape. This spread gives you a fresh perspective or offers a nudge in directions you may not have considered, while also highlighting patterns of the past you may want to avoid.

Mind, Body, Spirit

Tarot will never tell you to watch your cholesterol, but there are plenty of cards that relate to your well-being and growth—such as The Sun, Nine of Swords, and Four of Wands—making this a useful lens to look at your health from a holistic point of view. Pick three cards to tell you what you need to know about developing or healing your mind, body, and spirit. I was inspired by notes from my editor (*I love you, Julia!*) to do this spread right now. Here's what I pulled, along with my interpretations:

MIND—QUEEN OF COINS: It's time to get on top of your finances. Don't be afraid to ask uncomfortable questions about money matters because it is a growth edge that needs to be faced so you can evolve. (Note: This totally tracks as I'm separating and about to live on my own for the first time in twenty-five years!)

BODY—HIGH PRIESTESS: When it comes to your physical health, listen to your intuition because it's speaking to you. (Note: Again, this makes a lot of sense because the stress of separation is making my liver throb, and I need to check in with my doctor!)

SPIRIT—THREE OF WANDS: Plan the work so you can work the plan. Get moving in the direction of your goals knowing that baby steps count. (Note: Tarot for the win! I'm planning publicity for my first book as I edit this one, and it can be overwhelming, especially with everything else going on in my life. The reminder about baby steps is super helpful. Also, and this is where the "spirit" comes in, I went to a retreat and had an experience connecting with my inner child. A mantra that came out of that was her telling me: *Now we go*. The imagery of this card perfectly captures the essence of that message.)

Opportunities, Challenges, Outcomes

Like the Past, Present, Future spread, this can be as open-ended or specific as you want. Look for connections between the cards that identify any dynamics or narratives that can be opportunities or hindrances. Consider the story that these images are trying to tell in terms of the characters, colors, numbers, suits, positioning, or anything else that stands out.

When pulling three cards, I usually find the parameters above a bit too rigid because I'll end up trying to force meanings onto situations to make them make sense (of course, tarot totally trolled me with the Mind, Body, Spirit spread above!). Normally, I just ask, "What do I need to know about . . . ?" and let the cards determine their order as their story is revealed. If a more structured layout helps you give better readings, go for it! You're developing your own distinct style of tarot, so don't hesitate to go with a framework that aligns with your reading style or mood at that moment.

YOU DO YOU, BOO BOO
(PERMUTATIONS & IMPROVISATION)

There are hundreds of other spreads you can experiment with (we'll get to mine in a minute), or you can create your own. As I mentioned, the Celtic Cross is a "hell no" for me, but you may love it. Although this ten-card spread was first mentioned in A. E. Waite's *The Pictorial Key to the Tarot* in 1910, the Celtic Cross predates this iconic deck's creation and was likely used with regular playing cards before it was associated with tarot. You can easily find instructions for it online, so I won't get into it here (also, there aren't enough Tums in the world to get me through it).

A Card for Any Occasion

Try picking seven cards on Sunday night to give you guidance for the week ahead, or use two cards to represent the energy of both options in an either/or dilemma. You can align your reading with the cycles of the Moon, looking at how to create capacity under the Full Moon so you can manifest with the New Moon. Celebrate the changing seasons with a special tarot message to mark the Solstice or Equinox, or pull a card every week as a focal point for the coming days.

If you're a ritualistic reader, you can add an esoteric sense of ceremony to your birthday celebrations with a dedicated reading (even if it's a single card). I always suggest getting a tarot reading on your birthday because it's the start of *your* New Year, which makes the message more auspicious.

Let your reading be the subject of a painting or prompt for a poem. Your cards can help you heal old wounds, process intense emotions, and dare to dream bigger. Take a picture or journal about your reading so you have something to reflect on moving forward (messages that make no sense in the moment can become pertinent down the road). Or simply sit and meditate with the card that found you in this moment.

Love Readings

Relationship-specific spreads are having a moment with lots of people looking for guidance in affairs of the heart. Spreads concerning love are often five cards placed in a rainbow or cross formation (or any other shape that resonates).

If you're currently in a romantic relationship, each card in the layout is assigned to one of these positions (determine what they are before pulling cards): you, the other person, the relationship, the past, and the future. When it comes to the other person, you aren't spying on their energy because that's unethical (more on this in Chapter 7). Instead, you're looking at what you need to know about that person regarding your relationship or what you need to know in dealing with this person.

If you're single, a love spread can help you focus on what can be healed or looked at differently from your past, where you're at presently, what to consider that could help you be receptive to romance, and potential qualities or circumstances around your future partner. Each card is assigned to the following designations within the layout: past beliefs, past relationships, your current situation, what to focus on (this might have nothing to do with romance), and what is possible.

Avoid any spreads that claim to access another person's intentions or feelings about you because you're inviting a karmic kick in the ass when you dip into their energy uninvited.

Zodiac Reading

In astrology, there are twelve signs with distinct qualities and houses that concern different aspects of life. A traditional astrology-based tarot reading contains twelve cards in a circle that mirrors the zodiac wheel, with each card sitting in a different house. Cards are read in a counterclockwise direction around the wheel, starting at the nine o'clock position. What follows describes each card placement on the zodiac wheel and its areas of influence:

THE FIRST HOUSE (9, ARIES): Self, physical appearance, initiation, ignition, taking action.

THE SECOND HOUSE (8, TAURUS): Material security, resources, possessions, planting seeds.

THE THIRD HOUSE (7, GEMINI): Communication, expression, education, relating to others.

THE FOURTH HOUSE (6, CANCER): Home, family, foundations, emotional security, setting down roots.

THE FIFTH HOUSE (5, LEO): Creativity, leadership, romance, children, prominence, pleasure.

THE SIXTH HOUSE (4, VIRGO): Efficiency, systems, organization, productivity, physical health, good habits.

THE SEVENTH HOUSE (3, LIBRA): Balance, beauty, justice, committed partnerships.

THE EIGHTH HOUSE (2, SCORPIO): Money, power, sexuality, mental health, transformation, strategic investments.

THE NINTH HOUSE (1, SAGITTARIUS): Expansion, adventure, philosophy, travel, personal growth.

THE TENTH HOUSE (12, CAPRICORN): Career, ambition, discipline, responsibility, public roles.

THE ELEVENTH HOUSE (11, AQUARIUS): Innovation, philanthropy, quirkiness, community, collaboration.

THE TWELFTH HOUSE (10, PISCES): Intuition, compassion, subconscious, spirituality, sorrow.

Just as astrology reads the map of the sky to explore your journey through life, a tarot reading navigates the journey of self, and together they offer an incredibly thorough reading.

DIY Tarot (Design Your Own Spread)

Creating your own spread is easier than you think; don't hesitate to freestyle your own layout if you feel the urge. The only guidelines to keep in mind are arranging the spread in a way that resonates (circles, crosses, and arches are popular formations) and assigning an intention or influence to each position in the spread either before or as you pull the cards.

An example of intention within a four-card spread would be naming the spots as situation, obstacle, steps, and outcome. Areas of influence that can be referenced in a more overarching spread include career, romance, friendship, family, self-image, personal growth, health, travel, spirituality, community, or finances. When it comes to designing your spread, you're only limited by your creativity.

MY SPREAD

Anyone getting a tarot reading from me in the last thirty years has seen the same layout of twelve cards placed in a circle. This is the spread created and taught to me by my tarot mentor, Erica. It's rooted in astrology but has evolved over time into a more holistic exploration through every aspect of your life. It's a great example of how tarot evolves alongside the reader and also how imperative it is to intuitively refine your unique approach to the cards.

I no longer align my spread to astrology because it's taken on a life of its own. I read the cards in pairs across from one another, rather than going around one by one, and there isn't an assigned placement for a particular facet of life. As the reading progresses, the themes or areas of life reveal themselves.

This evolution of my reading style occurred because I was frustrated trying to wedge a card's meaning into specific parameters. We don't live our lives in silos such as romance, career, travel, etc. It's more like a fabric with intertwining threads that weave together to tell the story of you. This is how I view the relationship between the cards in my spread: The messages build upon one another in a multitude of ways to give you a sense of what's going on energetically in every aspect of your life. For example, when I pull The Moon and it advises you to protect your energetic boundaries by cutting etheric cords, that doesn't apply to just one part of your life. It may be more pronounced at work, but you would probably benefit from examining boundaries in your personal relationships as well.

As mentioned in Chapter 14, it's important to set an intention before you start pulling cards. You can state it out loud or keep it to yourself, but know why you're doing tarot at this moment. I recite the same statement to begin every reading and to set expectations and confirm intentions. Here is what I say:

I've laid the cards out in the spread, which is the pattern they're arranged in, and it serves as the framework for your reading. This spread looks like a clock: It's a circle with a card in each number position. We'll spend half of the time on this spread, and the rest of the time we'll split between pulling cards from the top and bottom of the deck, and you can ask any questions at the end. We're going to look at the cards in this spread across from one another in pairs, and as we go around the circle, it tells the story of you. But this isn't fortune-telling. I won't be saying you're going to meet Fred at Starbucks next Tuesday. You've drawn me a map, and I'm going to help you read it. You'll be getting a peek behind the curtain to see what's going on energetically from now to six-to-nine months out, and what you choose to do with this information is up to you because you have free will. If anyone claiming to be psychic says "If you don't do this, something terrible will happen . . ." it's bullshit. So that's my woo woo PSA. Are you ready?

Whether I'm pulling three cards or thirty, every reading will have a particular tone or vibe because tarot plugs into the other person's energy to deliver guidance in a way that resonates with the receiver.

A spread that is enveloped with emotional Cups and encouraging Wands has a very different feel compared to one that is strewn with heavy hitters from the Major Arcana. The insight can have a bossy or prescriptive quality, like a teacher assigning homework, or be gentle and encouraging guidance that feels like a hug from a caring friend. Maybe tarot delivers the no-nonsense, get-your-shit-together message you need to hear at that moment.

Every tarot spread—even three cards—can reveal a distinct flavor of the interpretation (e.g., no-nonsense versus lovey-dovey); take notice of these qualities if they become apparent to you. Picking up on the vibes of a particular reading (all business versus fun and flirty) is going to reveal the energetic fingerprint that will differentiate your tarot style from everyone else.

Two people can have the same cards in their spread and have completely different—yet totally relevant—readings because of many factors including geographic location, socioeconomic situation, relationship status, gender, age, race, and sexual expression, all of which play a role in how a reading will resonate. The message is universal, but the meaning is personal.

Experiment with different layouts (or create your own) to find a format that fits. And if a simple three-card spread does the job, that's great—it's what I use for events, and everyone leaves feeling like they received a very clear, accurate, and applicable reading.

A tarot reading is an act of service—you are a conduit being used for a higher purpose. The personal dialect you develop with your deck will imbue your readings with singular narratives that can be applied to any situation. We all access intuitive information differently, so take what works and leave the rest. Get readings from professionals to study their process. Incorporate methods from others, and make them your own.

The quality of your readings will soar once you apply your intuitive interpretation—that's where you find the magic of the cards and they start speaking to (and through) you. Your meaning of a card may not align with the so-called experts' interpretation, but it's yours and that makes it just as true as anyone else's definition. If the message of a card works within your tarot practice, the meaning is accurate. Take in the information that's available from others (including me), and let it inform your personal definition. This is how tarot becomes a powerful tool of spiritual self-discovery and personal empowerment.

A tarot deck is only as useful as the person wielding it. The cards can point out negative thought patterns, but breaking free from them is an inside job. Although tarot can highlight the path forward, only you can take the first step.

Tarot facilitates a conversation with your soul, guiding you to become the truest and best version of yourself.

The meaning of a card can embolden you to dream bigger and expect more. Tarot is your biggest cheerleader and sagest adviser—helping you learn from your mistakes and recognize opportunities.

During significant life transitions, you have the potential for transformation at every level—physical, emotional, spiritual, and energetic—but it's never easy and rarely comfortable. We're desperate for quick fixes and healing in equal measure, and while the cards can't provide predictions or guarantees, they can help you make sense of your distress as you navigate turbulent times.

Tarot's messages encourage you to let go of everyone else's agenda and start defining your worth on your terms. When you're questioning your purpose, hoping to Goddess there's more to life than what you're living, tarot offers the comfort or kick in the ass that you may not think you want, but most definitely need.

With tarot as your guide, you honor yourself. Heal yourself. Recognize yourself. You are reintroduced to yourself. This is what wisdom looks like. Welcome home.

Conclusion
∞

I work with tarot because it works.

On their own, tarot cards are pictures printed on paper, but when you put intention behind them and listen to the stories they have to tell, these seventy-eight pieces of paper can help you define desired outcomes, point out potential obstacles, and discover what's possible.

The symbolism of tarot contains the cosmic truth of the collective that we experience in a deeply personal way. When tarot is done well, space is created for a person to recognize their inner knowing and initiate their own healing. Tarot is a conduit to higher consciousness, and a single card can be a life-changing catalyst. Through the cards, you might give yourself permission to acknowledge and heal what has been denied or ignored—uncovering the gifts hidden within your wounds. The stories of the Major and Minor Arcana allow you to appreciate the lessons in your life and how they've woven together to bring you to this place.

If you put in the time and trust the process and the magic, your cards can bring clarity to any crisis. And with clarity comes freedom—often arriving in the form of life-altering decisions, such as leaving a relationship or embarking on a new career path. They can also assist you in the practical aspects of life (we all need to stop with the negative self-talk and meditate more). Whether you're navigating new chapters or just getting through your day, tarot is there to reassure and guide you every step of the way.

The cards shine a light on what has been hidden, and echo the lessons you have resisted, with a brutal honesty that is always in your best interest.

Tarot helps you know and accept yourself on a deeper level.

It is a privilege to witness someone's life through the lens of tarot. Thank you for allowing me to help you witness yours.

Acknowledgments
∞

I remember when my tarot deck, now worn and weathered, was shiny and untested (kind of like its owner). For a long time I couldn't articulate my fascination with the cards, or why I kept coming back to them regardless of where I was in my life. I now see tarot as my spiritual sidekick, guiding me along the path to my purpose and providing me with a career that is also a calling. And/but/also, the cards are only one character in this story. I am incredibly fortunate to have many beautiful souls in my corner—particularly during the writing and publication of this book, which coincided with an extremely challenging time in my life. These people offered their help, wisdom, guidance, and influence in ways I never expected and didn't realize I needed (#notthatkindofpsychic).

First up, the publishing coven: Thank you to my agent at Transatlantic, Alexandra D'Amico, for your immediate and enduring enthusiasm of this book (and the one that came before it). Your insight helped immensely and I can't wait to see what we conjure up next. I'm so fortunate to be with HarperCollins, and to have Julia McDowell as my editor. Thank you, Julia, for your astute questions and keen eye . . . and for coming in clutch with the title of this book! Rebecca Silver is my publicist and I wish everyone could experience a moment of her magic—thank you for your boundless efforts and enthusiasm. (We're going to make that patio happen, even if it's snowing.)

Thank you to Erica Von Kcaat for teaching me your witchy ways with a sense of humor, curiosity, and reverence that I aspire to in my own work. To Lori Bean for always being in my corner, pushing me to question who I am and challenging me to go for it. Lisa Anderson: You picked me up when I fell to pieces and there aren't enough words to convey my thanks. Treana Peake, for being my first (and favorite) tarot client from day one.

To Lisa Davis, Vanessa Gringer, and Yousra El Alaoui for keeping me accountable and holding my hand when I wobbled. Kari Lauritzen (and James and Mac), for being my chosen family and safe space. To Ronit Cohn for shouting my name in rooms of opportunity and helping me see beyond my wildest dreams. Eileen King, for reminding me I'm worth celebrating. Darren Wharrie: You are the ultimate sounding board, a true healer, and an exceptional human. Ryan Ostofe, thank you for your tough questions and unwavering belief in me. Brittany Ostofe: You are witchier than you realize and your authenticity inspires me daily.

Marissa Stapley: How we met was wildly cosmic and I'm grateful for your friendship and guidance. Trevor Frankfurt, for helping me celebrate like a pro and for our endless manifesting summits disguised as lunch dates. To Alex Seidel for your sage words and powerful magic. Asha Frost, your generosity and wisdom changed my trajectory. Maddox Lu for showing me that make-up isn't scary, we're never too old, and it's never too late. Sheri Trapler: Your artistry with hair helped me uncover my inner bombshell.

Nyakio Grieco, April Uchitel, Elizabeth Kott, Cyndi Finkle, Francesca Fartaj, Kat Gana, Christine Harris, Julie-Anne Lee, Emily Kratter, Jaymee Naik, Christina Pérez, Chela Reyna, Randy Schreck, and Prudence Jamieson—you have been instrumental in helping me write my next chapter. To all of my circle sisters: Knowing that I can reach out to you for reflection and support is a gift I don't take lightly—I'm so lucky to know you.

To Alanna McGinn, Jane McCann, Meredith Cox, MaryAnn DiMarco, Elena Sherwood, Wendy Alana, Kate King, Nicole Henderson, Kelsey Marie, Gwen Merrick, Stacey Sanderson, and Sasha Korper: Thank you for All Of The Things—you were more of a lifeline than you'll ever know.

My mom, Doris Parisan, and my sister, Shannon Beavis—thank you for showing up when I needed you most.

To my children (who are basically adults now, but will always be my babies): Thank you for your love and for letting me love you. You are both my favorite.

And finally, a massive THANK YOU to you, dear reader. You are also my favorite. I get to say "I am a professional tarot card reader, author, and speaker" because of you. Your support means the world to me and I love you very much.